Only Believe

Only Believe

Written and illustrated by
Georgina Fletcher

GSP

Only Believe
Georgina Fletcher

Published by Greyhound Self-Publishing 2015
Malvern, Worcestershire, United Kingdom.

Designed and Printed by Aspect Design
89 Newtown Road, Malvern, Worcs. WR14 1PD
United Kingdom
Tel: 01684 561567
E-mail: books@aspect-design.net
www.aspect-design.net

ISBN 978-1-909219-29-8

Contents

Foreword

It is my pleasure to introduce Georgina Fletcher to you, a recent arrival
to the ministry of writing. Georgina's writing has the benefit of a
wealth of human experience and this comes through on every page.
She not only has a wide breadth of life-experiences, some of which
are quite harrowing, but more importantly, every experience has been
turned into an opportunity to grow in her faith in God. Georgina has a
very uncomplicated and straightforward trust in God, to her God will
always be what he says he will be. You will smile at some of the stories,
maybe even laugh, but some will move you emotionally. Georgina is
a remarkable lady, she has turned obstacles into opportunities and her
life is a shining witness to her great God. May the story you now read
help you in the challenges you face on your journey.

Jim Dick
Retired pastor and member of Georgina's local church

Introduction

Have you ever wondered where the end of the rainbow is? Are you in a dark place where the sun never seems to shine? Maybe you are so self-assured you have no interest in what the future holds. Some of you say 'Whatever will be, will be, the future is not ours to see.' Where is your position in the journey of life? Are you travelling light or weighed down with baggage? Do you know where you are heading or have you no sense of direction?

My position was at the back of the queue, with too much baggage and too little sense! Fear and negativity escorted me on my travels, with anxiety stamped on my ticket. Anyone who has ever read or is familiar with John Bunyan's book *Pilgrim's Progress* will understand it is about a person who embarks on a soul-searching adventure, encountering many obstacles and characters along the way. In the Bible, Jesus says 'wide is the path that leads to destruction, and narrow is the path that leads to life, but few will find it.' *Only Believe* covers my own personal journey from childhood to present day, unearthing potholes, obstacles, treasure and promises. The journey is in three stages:

1. A journey of aimless wanderings with despair holding me in its grip.

2. A journey of discovery with hope giving me a helping hand.

3. My journey leads me to faith where I can at last relax and enjoy the view!

My journey is not yet over and there may be more obstacles to face, but now I am travelling in the right direction with an amazing travelling companion, his name is Jesus! My hope is that it will encourage and inspire you through your own journey of life. This world needs confirmation and assurance that there *is* a purpose for its existence, and there *is* a future that *is not* bleak and hopeless. *Only Believe!*

In the words of Jesus, 'Do not be afraid, only believe,' (Mark 5:36).

Chapter One
My Journey Begins

When I was a child I was called Dilly-Daydream because I spent most of my time day-dreaming! I loved reading books, and would often imagine myself as one of the characters from the stories; this is what kids do. I was a small child with a big imagination and songs like 'Somewhere Over the Rainbow' fascinated me. Stories that began with 'Over the hills and far away' often made me wonder what *was* over those hills. I was born and brought up in Malvern, so this gave me an excellent opportunity to explore the Malvern Hills. At five years of age they towered above my tiny frame, each hill was like a giant to me.

I was a child growing up in the 1950s. It was a hard time for most people after the previous decade of war. My parents moved from the city to the country believing their quality of life would improve. Previously they had lived in the heart of Birmingham; the war had destroyed everything they had, so they moved to Malvern to run the Beauchamp Hotel (now called the Great Malvern Hotel). I have three older sisters, the elder two were born in the city and my other sister and I were born in Malvern. This is where my journey begins. My eldest sister was only a toddler when she suffered brain damage after a bomb exploded near their home. She let go of our mother's hand as they were hurrying to get to an air-raid shelter. It all happened so quickly, our poor mum, what she must have gone through when she realised her little one was missing. It was understandable to see why they moved. They had to begin from scratch, as did scores of other families after the war. We were not well off, but we never lacked anything. Both my parents worked jolly hard just to feed and clothe their four daughters. Father was strict, but not cruel, and mother was a warm, positive person. Her favourite saying was 'Do not say the word *can't*!' She was always reminding me, 'Take the *t* away and you *can* do anything today!' Sadly her words fell on deaf ears as my vivid imagination turned ugly, attracting all sorts of fears throughout childhood. Spiders, heights, dentists, doctors, lifts, the dark, you name it, I was afraid of it! You might be thinking that most children are afraid of those things, but they became phobias to me, along with many other things. *Phobia: an irrational fear of people, places and things.*

Do you remember the bogeyman? The bogeyman was a figment of most children's imagination during the 1950s and that is what it was—bogus, non-existent—but in my mind he lived wherever I placed him; the cupboard under the stairs, the attic, the bottom of the garden and the cellar. Anywhere that was hard to get at or hidden away. Many parents at that time would use the bogeyman as a weapon with their children, saying, 'If you are naughty the bogeyman will get you!' This was not the case with my parents, as they did not believe in scaring their children with such nonsense. However, I continued to carry round with me a great sense of danger, fear and anxiety.

My earliest recollections of childhood are a little vague, but I do remember the hair washing days. I simply hated having my hair washed! I would choose a different place to hide each time that dreaded day came. My mother, bless her, always found me. She would drag me from under the bed or from behind the curtain ignoring my cries of protest. Then she carried on the task in hand with a firm, but kind, manner. The thought of water on my head petrified me, so learning to swim was not a fun activity to pursue. Our uncle would come all the way from Birmingham to teach us girls to swim; he was a keen outdoor enthusiast, so encouraged us to be the same. He took us to Tewkesbury swimming baths, on what was to be my first and last visit, due to an elderly man having a heart attack and dying at the pool. It was a shocking thing for young eyes to witness, so I never did learn to swim.

My father at the Beauchamp Hotel (where I was born) now called the Great Malvern Hotel.

I was also a sickly child, catching every ailment that was around. This brought me lots of fuss and attention, which my little mind loved. This, in turn, caused me to invent other ailments. One day, mother took me to the doctor and I overheard him telling her I may be a hypochondriac. I walked out of that place chuffed to bits thinking I had some important illness! *Hypochondriac: a person who is over anxious about their health.*

My next memory was of starting school. In those days, we did not have the privilege of pre-school, so I was not prepared at all. It was in a grand old building, but to me it was big, dark and scary,

My sisters, aunt, uncle, and baby nephew. I am the one hiding in my mother's arms.

though what I found most unbearable were the school dinners. The menu only seemed to consist of boiled mince and watery cabbage; the smell was so nauseating I wondered how I would survive! The dinner ladies resembled Mrs Trunchball from the film *Matilda*, and held their ladles like weapons shouting 'What did you say?' In the film, *Oliver* the little boy dares to ask for more, but in my school it was the opposite. If any of us kids dared to say, 'Please, miss, I don't want any more,' we were in trouble! So at home, I would wail and moan until my mother eventually gave in and agreed for me to take packed lunches. This made it hard for her as she worked long hours and had little time to prepare evening meals. The school dinner was supposed to be my main meal of the day. I was a very fussy and finicky eater when I was little, living mainly on tomato soup!

With both parents working full-time, our older sister looked after us. She did everything in that home: cooking, washing and cleaning; then she met and married a very nice man and moved out to do the same in her new home! That is what it was like back then, simple, but safe. Both myself and my other sisters missed her so much as she had been like a second mum to us. A ten-year-old was still a child, not like these days when children are exposed to everything and anything around them. I was a very nervous, shy child, with incredibly low self-esteem. I could not even spell my own name correctly. I dreaded catching buses, and crossing a busy road brought me out into a sweat! I wore fear like a garment. Everything was a chore not a challenge. Everything was a burden not a blessing. Nowadays, one would seek specialist help, but not back in the fifties and sixties. The fears became more crippling as I emerged from childhood into my teen years and adulthood. Worry was my middle name. Negativity escorted me throughout life and anxiety waited for me on the doorstep!

No wonder I suffered with anxiety with a hairstyle like this!

School days were tough for me. To get to my local primary school I had to go through a lane, and continue along a side road. Both my parents and sisters took me when they could, but this was not possible every day. Along that side road there was always somebody waiting to knock me over and call me names. Tearing my books, taking my lunch, you name it, they did it. The teachers at school were not concerned when I told them. I did not like to tell my parents as they were busy all the time, but when my uniform was torn, out it all came. My mother was livid! I had never seen her like that before. The next day she took me by the hand and marched me into school. Everybody was looking, I started thinking this was not a good idea. I had mixed feelings, proud of my mum, but afraid of the kids.

The headmistress did not take kindly to my mother's entrance, but did assure her that she would deal with the culprits (though this never happened.) Life got unbearably worse for me after that day, to such an extent that I had to move schools. I liked my new school as it smelt of fresh paint and pine wood! I began making friends, something that had been difficult for me before. I was not academic, but did work hard. This was because even though fear had a grip on me—it was fear that drove me on. Fear of failing caused me to become a perfectionist later in life, this in turn developed into frustration, as I could never reach the desired result.

Can you identify with this? Are you in the place of wanting everything to be right but never quite getting there?

I believed I was ugly, so I would wear too much make-up. I believed I was overweight, so I would not eat properly. This resulted in me developing bulimia, in my late teens/early twenties. *Bulimia: an eating disorder characterised by the person overeating, afterwards forcing themselves to be sick.* I used to eat in front of people (to be sociable) then go and be sick in the toilet. I would run the taps and pull the chain (no modern flush!) to block out the noise. It is amazing how nobody was aware what was going on, it was like a secret disease I could not share with anyone. It was not until I went into nursing a few years later that I recovered from bulimia. I was on night duty and so hungry! At mealtimes we had to depend on the vending machine, with its limited choice of foods for our meals. One night there was only a choice of egg or chicken sandwiches. I had never been partial to either, but I was so hungry I had double portions! My hunger outweighed my performance that night. Now remember this sentence!

Back then, I craved for people's approval, so I would go out of my way to gain friendships. I was so naive and did not realise I was giving the wrong impression to some of my friends. I was a teenager during the 1960s and sex had exploded on the scene. There was no

booklet on the subject and I did not fully comprehend the man/ woman thing. This resulted in a major incident causing me to be emotionally scarred for years to come. I was gang-raped at only seventeen years of age. The saddest thing about it was that I thought they were my friends. How wrong I was. I included sex in my long list of fears after that painful ordeal.

My mother and sisters supported me throughout the following months. But mother kept saying, 'Don't tell your dad. Don't tell your dad.' No charges or publicity were made. Everything stayed hush-hush. These days it is exposed and uncovered, but not back then. We just papered over the cracks of our pain and carried on with our lives as if nothing had happened. The emotional and physical memory of that awful day stayed in the recesses of my mind; nightmares plagued me for a long time. I have heard that the mind can be compared to a tape recorder and presses playback as often as it likes. This was certainly true for me. With just my own strength, I could not overcome my fears, pain and endless anxieties, so I continued my journey through life by putting on a brave face. When I left school, I worked for a time as a sales assistant in a large department store; then secured a promotion to deputy manageress of a smaller retail firm. Chains of boutiques were springing up all over the UK and I wanted to be part of this trendy fashion scene. I did not like the drugs, sex and rock and roll of that period, but it did not stop me loving the clothes! Top names like Jean Shrimpton, Vidal Sassoon and Twiggy gave us a look that made us feel good on the outside, but not on the inside. Girls that I knew were already thin, should they get any thinner? In my mind, I falsely believed I was overweight, but found it difficult to stick to a diet. My love of sweet stuff was hard to lose. Being sick after eating seemed the only option to me, so I would still suck the chocolate then spit it all out. What a sad place to be, but that was the only place I knew at the time.

A few years later, my dad became quite ill and developed

Parkinson's disease. He was twenty years older than mother and she herself was not well. All the years of working so hard just to provide the basics for her family had taken its toll on her. My sister suffered brain damage from the effects of a bomb blast when she was a toddler; remember when I said she got lost in the mad rush to the air-raid shelter? When searching amongst the rubble, they found her barely alive. There was no healthcare or day facilities like there are now, and no disability allowances to make life easier. My two other sisters were married and had children of their own. I remained at home trying to help mother in her role as a carer as well as working full time. This I found difficult. After dad took early retirement due to ill health, mum continued working part-time while looking after him and my sister. She would sometimes ask me to keep an eye on him, and often I would find him asleep still holding a lit cigarette in that favourite armchair of his. That armchair was covered in cigarette butts. Eventually his illness got so severe he had to go into a nursing home, and within a few years dad passed away. Mother developed stomach cancer not long after his death; it was a very upsetting time for the family. It made me start questioning my existence, 'What is the purpose of living? Why all the suffering? Where was the end of the rainbow?'

I started dabbling in spiritualism. It was not intentional, a friend invited me to a meeting, but, thank God, I did not like it at all. None of it made sense, much of it was spooky; I used to come away from those meetings with more fears than before! Mother had to undergo a major operation, but she made an amazing recovery. Her warmth, optimism and steely determination made me feel ashamed. 'Why can't I be like my mother?' I thought. 'Why do I always fail at everything?' I believed I was useless and convinced myself I was overweight and ugly. My mind held the information on file under the heading 'hopeless case'. In reality it is not about the size, weight or height we are, but about how comfortable we feel about ourselves. True beauty is God-given *not* media-led, as I discovered years later. My sisters were my source of encouragement, no matter how bad I felt about myself. One of them was a hairdresser and she would style my hair so beautifully, but despite their best efforts, I still remained a shy young thing. I secretly admired their way of life with nice homes and lovely children.

Life goes on, as the saying goes, so back on went that brave face as I continued my journey. I started thinking if I could work in a place where I could help others, it would take my mind off my pain. I applied for nursing training in South Devon. It was difficult to leave my mum and my sisters as we were a close-knit family, but I needed to get away. I kept thinking, 'Out of sight, out of mind' (how wrong I was). My plan was to train in both psychiatry and general nursing.

The psychiatric hospital was a huge old building set in acres of ground on the edge of Dartmoor. The nurse's home, where I would stay for the next few years, was in those grounds. This, to, was very big and set on a hill. Inside there was dark panelled wood everywhere and really high ceilings. As I approached it, panic set in and I started thinking I had made a mistake in leaving the comfort of my family. I arrived on a Sunday along with a handful of others, and after a very brief introduction, were shown to our rooms. The breathtaking view from my window made up for the size, a box room with just enough space for the single bed and small wardrobe! After a restless night, we all had to report to the nurse's college, where I met other young nervous students. We were all in it together, not knowing what to expect, and that eased my fears a little. There was a three-month intense study programme, and afterwards we were to spend part of the week doing practical nursing on the wards. Psychiatry in those days was *very* different to now, back then everybody seemed to be bunched together in one place, but identified by three different headings: psychosis, neurosis, and mentally handicapped.

Our first teaching session began with writing a list of the symptoms under each heading. As we were copying the list for neurosis from the blackboard, I realised I could identify with the symptoms! The tutor teaching us explained that people with any form of neurosis find it difficult to cope with the stresses and strains of everyday living. 'That sounds like me,' I thought, shifting uncomfortably in my seat. I started thinking maybe I should be a patient and not the nurse, but when the tutor went on to tell us that it was common for anybody to have just a few of those symptoms, I felt much better—although it did make me realise I had some issues that seriously needed sorting out. But how? I dared not approach the staff, as I was afraid they would tell me to leave, so I carried on in a typical British manner, hiding behind that mask. My social life was spent dabbling in the occult; the nurses seemed to love anything dark and gothic: séances, tarot cards and Ouija boards. Then I stumbled onto the art of lying, and realised this could be a way of gaining acceptance without actually participating in stuff I did not want to do. Lying became my survival kit. When the cigarette that smelt like urine and wet grass was passed round the room, and it was my turn to inhale, I would pretend to smoke it saying, 'Mmmm, nice!' I did a similar thing with the tarot cards. I would say something they wanted to hear and folk would lap it up! Amazingly, I never indulged in any of those things for real. Lying, of course, had to leave me. Which it did when I met and married a man whom I thought would be my ticket to freedom.

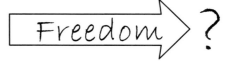

I met him while studying at the college, he seemed different from the crowd and we shared many interests. I thought I was in love, but in reality I was not ready for a relationship. He was the first kind man that I had ever met, and I mistakenly thought he could look after me and free me from my insecurities. We both agreed to get our careers established before even thinking of having children. We moved out of the nurse's home to rent a small cottage nearby.

I had a beautiful black poodle called Pepsy, who had lived with my mother in Malvern while I did my training; so I decided to bring her to the cottage to live with us. Pepsy was an elderly dog, and in hindsight I realised I should not have moved her as she became ill shortly after arriving at the cottage. She developed diabetes and lost the sight in one eye. She required lots of practical care; it broke my heart to see her suffering. We also had a tabby cat called Tibby who was brought with the intent to keep the local rats at bay! She was a large straggly cat that spent most of her time outdoors, but once Pepsy came on the scene, she rarely left her side. At first Pepsy would snap at Tibby and even bite her, but Tibby was not in the

Tibby in the snow.

least bit bothered. Eventually, they became so close they shared the same bed, so we had to buy a bigger basket! After Pepsy died, Tibby still slept in that basket.

The first few years of our marriage were good, but after I passed my exams and became a qualified nurse, tensions rose between us. My heart was not in nursing anymore, I longed to go back into the fashion industry. I was still Dilly-Daydream thinking one day I could be a model or fashion designer! Standing only five-foot-two tall, a career in modelling would remain a dream; but fashion design, could I do it? My husband was kind enough to let me pursue my dream and supported me when I enrolled in the local art college. Looking back now, I realise I made a big mistake in making that choice. I loved being an art student and made some nice friends, but I lost sight of the fact that I was a married woman. The fashion industry can be a desirable but pretentious place to be. One can get lost amongst the glittering, frivolous trappings, which suited my character at that time very well. I was still living in a make-believe world that I had created for myself. If only I knew then what I know now, I would have given it all up, but I did *not* know. My husband wanted our marriage to work, but I was married to my work! I was often working long late hours at college, which was not a good recipe for a young couple. He began seeking comfort elsewhere. As you may have guessed, the marriage ended in divorce after only three years. A year prior to this we had purchased a two-bed terraced house in a village on the edge of Dartmoor. He moved back into the residential home at the hospital and agreed for me to stay at the house until I had finished my college course.

This is an outfit I made in my first year at college.

Chapter Two
Confusion

My journey through life continued to take me on my own self-destructive path with all its baggage. After the divorce, I accepted the blame. Although at the time I really believed it was not my fault. I always thought I was the victim of life's cruel plan.

Do you understand what I mean, do you feel like you are a victim?

After three years, I obtained a diploma in fashion design, and instead of thinking it through, I set up in partnership with a friend. We thought we could be the next Laura Ashley, but our ignorance cost us our time, money and even our friendship. So 'gullible' was thrown in with the rest of my baggage!

I carried on with the party girl act, mixing with the fake and the frivolous, but it was so artificial and I was heading nowhere. Deep down inside, my heart was breaking, but I did not understand why. Nothing around me and nobody I met could fill that sense of emptiness I carried round with me. Did you know that the word *void* is a noun? This means that it is an actual place and it resembles a vacuum. Man throughout the ages has tried to fill this vacuum, this void inside of us. It is within every human being, giving them the desire to be needed, loved and valued. We look for love in all the wrong places and marry for all the wrong reasons, then end up with a *decree nisi* (divorce paper) and begin our search again! The same goes for money. We buy things we do not really need and spend what we do not have, then end up with a pile of debts and the bailiffs at our door. We take out loans and second mortgages; we crave for the biggest car and the latest gadgets; we spend a fortune on clothes and toiletries to make us look, smell and feel good; and *still* we feel empty inside. Our lives seem to be one long journey looking for bigger, better and brighter things, and we never seem satisfied until we find them. Whatever happened to contentment, appreciation and thankfulness?

Do you get excited about the latest technology? Are you a shopaholic? Do you spend hours online buying stuff you don't really need?

Only the one creator God, who designed this amazing universe, can fill that void in our lives. Look no further as he *is* the real thing! God has created all of us to be complete in him. First, we have to allow God entry into our lives and believe in his existence, to find out his plan and purpose for each of our lives. That sense of emptiness inside of us is because we need to know the truth. A car with no fuel inside it will not move at all. A person with no food inside them will develop symptoms, after a long time they can die. It is impossible to function efficiently and maintain a balanced life without knowing the truth. Back then, I had not grasped this reality. I stumbled through life with a blindfold on, not knowing what was going to happen next.

At a party, I met a man who was handsome, charming and confident, and I did not want to lose him. Could he be my knight in shining armour who would take me over the hills and far away, I wondered. I was still living within the confines of my childish dreams and had not yet emerged into the real world. I was an escapist and a dreamer. Life had dealt me a nasty blow, so I did not want to live there. I was surprised when this man took an interest in me, but pleased that he did! It was one of those whirlwind romances that you see on the films. However, it did not turn out to be a happy ever after story where the couple ride off into the sunset on a white horse! Once we were married, life came knocking at our door in the form of debt. Now money had never been a real issue with me. My mother taught us girls the true value of money saying, 'The poorest person can save just a penny a week.' We started married life with excess baggage, he brought his own set of fears to join mine and debt was one of them. I was still longing for security and had a need to be loved (remember that void?)

We joined in matrimony for all the wrong reasons, and fumbled through the relationship with its already fractured foundation. Although we did care for one another in our own way, and he made me laugh, which is something I hardly ever did before. We both loved animals, our place was home to two cats (Tibby included!), one rabbit and a dog. We moved from Devon to Bristol and bought a little terraced house.

Life was good to begin with. We both worked full-time, but still managed to decorate our home and make the garden look nice. My husband was the gardener, not me, I was the one who appreciated it when all the hard work was done! His mother often came to stay with us during the early years of our marriage. This I found difficult as she was constantly finding fault in my ability to do anything right. In her eyes, I was not good enough for her son. In my eyes, I did not feel I was good enough for anyone. I so wanted her to like me, so I did everything I could think of to make her accept me. There was more give than take on my part in the mother–daughter-in-law relationship, but it was worth it. She gradually warmed towards me, especially after we gave her grandchildren. Oh, how she adored those boys!

Before babies came along, my husband and myself often went to the local pub for the occasional drink. He loved his pint of beer, but no more than anyone else, I thought. Then he started bringing alcohol home with him after work. This fuelled anger in him that I had never witnessed before. I saw a different person to whom I had married. At first, I tried to understand his outbursts of temper, but he often blamed me for anything that went wrong. If I tried to defend my side of the argument, it made matters worse, so I let him have the last say and clung to the saying 'Anything for a quiet life' which gave me comfort. There were times when he became abusive, both physically and verbally. This was more than I could bear, as I did not know what to do. The crazy thing was that when he was sober he was a nice person. He was always sorry for what he had done, but neither of us sought professional help. So we continued aimlessly on our journey together, with me secretly wondering if I would ever find the end of the rainbow.

My thoughts turned to having a baby. I so longed for a child of my own. Surely a child would make our lives complete? We talked it through and agreed to start a family. For a time things got better. He stopped drinking at home and turned the spare room into a nursery, but life was still my enemy and threw complications in our way. I was so thrilled when tests revealed I was pregnant, but within a few months I suffered a miscarriage which left me heartbroken. This same cycle continued over the next few years, and after three traumatic miscarriages, we were both left devastated. My husband began drinking heavily again, and I was an emotional mess. We started blaming one another, without having proper tests done, but eventually saw a specialist who informed me I only had one working fallopian tube. There was a very slim chance of conception, but not impossible. The specialist advised us not to raise our hopes. Hope, what was that? I thought. Hope was an alien concept to me as my life at the time was full of worry, fear and negativity.

But life does not stand still so we made every effort to make the marriage work, despite our serious issues. Then I got pregnant again, was this possible? Could the baby in my womb really be mine this time? The consultant ordered me to have complete bed rest after I survived the first three months of my pregnancy. The firm that I was working for allowed me to be an outworker, doing sewing in my home, but eventually I had to give up this job. One of my neighbours kept me company when she could and eventually became a good friend. During those months, she shared her faith in Jesus with me. I had always thought there was a God out there somewhere, but had never taken the time to find out where! Her God sounded different and real. I started having mixed up emotions

and did not know why. I was challenged on many an occasion by my neighbour, but would miss her if she did not call.

Well, those six months soon went, and it seemed like a miracle to reach full term, but my neighbour had been praying for me! I went into hospital early due to false contractions. They decided to keep me in overnight and allowed me to walk around, which was great after months of bed rest, so I took a walk along the hospital corridor and noticed a door marked chapel. It was slightly open, and out of curiosity,

I went in. I did not know what I was expecting. Nobody was in there so I sat down. The stillness made me cry. I cried for ages until there were no tears left. I cannot remember exactly what I said, I just cried out to God to help me keep this baby. It was a cry of sheer desperation from my heart.

Chapter Three
Life and Death

I knew nothing back then about the one and only true God, I knew nothing about this God sending his son, Jesus, to die for the entire human race. I had no idea that this God, who had designed and created the entire universe, wanted to know me personally and adopt me into his family. He wants a living, breathing relationship with us. Is that awesome or what? At the time, I was not aware of any of this. He had heard the cry of my heart despite me not knowing him on a personal level. I held in my arms a beautiful baby boy. My husband and I attempted to settle our differences to enjoy our son.

Having a baby definitely changes a person's life. I stopped being so preoccupied with my own shortcomings and started enjoying our precious baby. I did not have a clue how to raise an infant, so went to the library to collect as many books as I could! Our baby's first Christmas was ours too, because this was the first Christmas my husband was sober. One evening our neighbour invited us, a family of three, to her home. My husband would not go, but I did. I met some of her church friends, who did their best in answering the many questions I fired at them. That night I asked Jesus to come into my life. I did not understand everything straight away, but I *did* start having a sense of purpose in my existence, also one of my fears left that day; the fear of death. That night I just *knew* heaven was a very real place and one day I would see it! Good, one fear gone, I thought, but what about the other hundred? *Keep reading and all will be revealed!* I started remembering other people who had talked to me about Jesus. When I worked at the hospital, a nurse said to me, 'I am praying for you.' At the time, I did not have a clue what she was on about, but I am glad she did! When I first moved to Bristol, I worked in a clothing factory for a short time, and whilst there I met a girl who told me how Jesus had changed her life. We kept in touch and eventually became very good friends.

If you are a Christian, please continually pray for your friends and family. Share with them how Jesus has turned your life around.

This pram was used
for all four of my boys.

I often wonder if it was not for those friends that prayed for me, and those people who shared their story with me, where would I be today? I am so grateful to them all. Though when I first asked Jesus into my life I did not understand the full picture of *why* Jesus had died on that cross. The death, burial and resurrection of Jesus was still a mystery to me. It was not until many years later that the picture unfolded and became a beautiful reality in my life. My husband did not seem to mind when I told him, but my sisters thought I had gone 'All religious' and were quite concerned. I started going to my neighbour's church and was soon involved in the various activities there. I took my lovely baby with me too. My husband presented himself well to the church folk, and often came on special occasions. Nobody knew what was going on behind the four walls of our home. My husband loved our baby son very much, but he found the stresses and strains of everyday living difficult. Drinking to excess was his only way of coping. Handling problems scared both of us. We did not cope in a mature, responsible way because we were not mature, responsible people! I would cry and moan and he would resort to drink. What a pair!

Is this what you do? Do you have issues going on behind the four walls of your home?

In the spring of the second year of our baby's life, my journey was about to get very hard and I was totally unprepared for it. I received news that my mother was very ill. When I saw her, it was apparent that she was dying. She had developed pneumonia and was in a semi-coma. Drifting in and out of this coma, she refused to go to hospital. 'That's my Mum, determined to the end!' I thought. She had to have oxygen for her breathing and was doubly incontinent; it was so distressing to see our mother like this. She had always been so full of life and had cared for her precious daughters, now it was our turn to care for her.

My sisters and I took it in turns to wash, feed and comfort our wonderful mother; making her as comfortable as possible. I knew nothing about praying for the sick in those days. I was ignorant of my new position in Jesus Christ. However, what little I did know, I wanted to share with my mum. The night it was my turn to sit by mum's bedside I took the opportunity to tell her the truth, that Jesus is the son of God and if she believed this in her heart she would have eternal life (never die but live forever with Jesus!). I shared with her that I was not afraid of dying because I knew where

I was going; mum feebly held out her hand to me, so I put my hand in hers. Her hand was icy cold. She did not utter a word but her eyes lit up and her mouth curled up into a sort of smile. It was her way of telling me she knew the truth. I felt an amazing warmth go through my body, something I had never experienced in my life before. Within a few days she passed from this earth into Jesus' arms. Death no longer had a hold on her. Our mother, though she was only in her early sixties, was now free and dancing in heaven!

After the funeral, life went on as usual. Even though I knew mum was safe and happy, I still missed her terribly. My husband was exceptionally understanding during my time of grief, so when I was invited to a Christian event, he said, 'You go along, it will do you good' so I did. I remember that Saturday in April so clearly, it was a Christian celebration. I did not realise Christians could have so much fun and joy, there were lovely songs and dancing with flags and streamers. Everybody sang and danced to God; they were thanking him for his son, Jesus. I could see they loved Jesus very much. I did not have that love for him and wondered why. I had been a Christian for nearly a year and still not opened the book! I planned to find out more about Jesus through reading this book, the Bible. Sadly, this did not happen straight away, as more heartbreak was about to come my way.

My mother and her brother in their early twenties.
They are both now in heaven dancing with Jesus!

Chapter Four
Help!

It was late when I arrived home after the celebration. It was very rare for me to go out like that, but I did enjoy myself. My husband greeted me in the downstairs hall saying, 'Don't check on our baby as I have settled him for the night.' I had never been apart from him before, but I was tired, so off we went to bed. The next morning I woke earlier than usual and the sun was streaming through the curtains.

My husband was still asleep; he always had a lie-in on Sundays while I went to church. I could not wait to hold my baby boy and hurried into the nursery, but was not prepared for what I was about to see. Fear gripped me so hard I began to shake. My heart was racing and my mind was screaming, though I did not make a sound. My baby, my beautiful baby's face, was a mass of bruises. I picked him up and cuddled him close to me. I did not know Jesus as I do now. Words like 'hope' and 'faith' were still a mystery to me. I wanted to cry but was afraid my husband would wake up, so I just let out a faint, 'Help me, Jesus.' I decided to go early to church and get help there.

I sat with my baby for a very long time in the pastor's office; he was extremely patient and kind to me while I told him my story in floods of tears! He admitted he had never witnessed anything like this before, and suggested we call a doctor to check the baby was okay. By this time, my baby had woken up and seemed his usual happy self! I was so relieved, but my main concern was what to do next. I was afraid to go home and face my husband. I was so naive and had no idea what would happen when the authorities came on the scene. This is what did happen: the emergency doctor was called out; our baby was admitted to hospital; Social Services were contacted and had various meetings with my husband and myself; and the powers that be kept me in hospital for a week with my baby.

My husband would not take responsibility for the incident at first, but later admitted it got too much for him. He was a broken man and started realising he had a serious problem. However, I found it very hard to understand this at the time, so I added unforgiveness and guilt to my baggage that day. My poor baby, I was so overwhelmed with guilt for not being there to protect him.

The outcome from all this was horrendous. Our precious baby went into short-term care for about six months. To me it seemed forever, I could not take it all in. They broke the news to us while we were at the hospital, so I asked if I could spend my last hour alone with my  baby. This time I did not go to the chapel. It was a lovely sunny day, so I found a quiet corner in the hospital grounds. I began crying out to God, 'Well, God, you answered my cry for help when I so longed for a baby and gave me a beautiful son. I do not understand what is happening, or what to do, so I ask you to look after my baby and let the people who look after him be kind to him. Please bring him back to me very soon.' Then it was time for them to take my baby from me.

The pain was unbearable. I cannot begin to describe it, I felt nothing, I had nothing, I *was* nothing. I was so broken up inside and did not function properly for days. My husband felt so guilty and made every effort to make amends. Despite what he had done, he was hurting too, but I was blinded by my own pain and found it difficult to respond to him. I was very fragile, but life does not stand still, so I attempted to keep going and stay sane to get our baby back. I did not experience the closeness or comfort of Jesus as I do now (years later!) *but he was there*! He was with me through all my years of pain, never leaving my side. What Jesus was doing in my life was amazing, but I was not aware of it at first. Nineteen months previously, when I had asked Jesus into my life, a glimmer of hope had come alive in me. This hope was like a seed that needed to grow. My seed had not grown very much because I had not taken the time to encourage its growth. By reading God's message (the Bible), praying and spending time with Jesus, this 'hope seed' would

grow stronger and develop into faith. I had not done any of these things, but God was still there for me and he was *not* going to let me go!

This is how God answered the second cry from my heart; our baby son was sent to a foster family for a period of four to six months, but for some reason unknown to any of us, it did not work out, so he went to another family and this time it did. They were a young Christian couple with two small children of their own, and were absolutely marvellous with our baby! My husband and I were able to visit as often as we liked and our baby always looked happy, well fed, and contented. God had responded to my prayer!

My husband began seeking help for his drink problem, though still would not accept he could be an alcoholic. This was a small breakthrough and a big relief because I was expecting our second baby, so it was good seeing him making the effort to get help. We both agreed to have marriage counselling, which we attended for several months. My husband even made the commitment to become a Christian, but some folk questioned the validity of this, believing he had only done it to keep our babies. Well, for right or wrong reasons, he did change for the better, and life was calmer without him drinking. Our firstborn came back to us only a month before our second baby was born! It was like having twins as they were only eighteen months apart in age. Twin buggies had recently arrived in the shops, so I was able to purchase one, which made getting around much easier!

We moved to a larger house and to a church where there were young families with children. We got involved in the life of the church, and things looked promising for a while. My husband went out most evenings to the church meetings while I stayed home to look after our boys. I began listening to tapes (CDs had not been invented then!) of lovely praise and worship music when the boys had gone to bed.

However, it was not long before my husband would come home

at night smelling of drink. At first, I did not take much notice, but when it happened week after week, I questioned him about it. He became abusive towards me, and said he had been having an affair. When he woke the next day, he realised what he had done and was sorry for his actions, but still admitted to the affair. I was still struggling with insecurities of my own, now this. I did not know how much more I could take.

We sought help at the church and they said we should stay together and resolve our differences for the sake of the children. They gave us jobs to do in the church, my husband helped run the bookstall and I worked in the Sunday school. We continued like that for a few years giving God lip service by praying, singing and listening to the preacher, but never fully understanding the song, prayer or teaching. The rest of the week, we lived as the world does: working, watching television, eating, sleeping. I found it hard to trust my husband, so how could I trust God? I still had not opened the Bible for answers. Things were going on within the four walls of our home that the elders of the church were not aware of. My anxieties got worse and I began living in fear of my husband. I started thinking it would be calmer for the boys if we lived apart, but he did not agree. He even threatened to take them from me for good. What could I do? I allowed fear to control my actions.

When it got bad at home I would ring the police while he was sleeping in a chair (drunk). The police were always reluctant to come into our house when I called them. In the 1980s, domestic violence was not taken as seriously as it is now. The police would turn up at the house, but stay outside; the only assistance I received was a lift to a women's refuge. This happened more than once and each time we went to a different refuge. Staying in those refuges opened my eyes to the suffering all around me. I was so naive, as I had not been aware of their existence until I became a victim of abuse myself. Everything was hush-hush and hidden away. Sometimes a social worker would take us to them with just an overnight bag. I was always too afraid to collect our belongings in case my husband woke up. I felt terrible putting our sons through this as they were so young, both under five years old, but I did it to protect them. Some of the refuges were shabby and unwelcoming, but not all. Many of the women first appeared hostile and defensive, but once they realised I was not a threat, they shared their stories with me. These women were literally hiding for their lives, no wonder they were suspicious of me at first. They were living under the shadow of death threats and extreme violence from their abusers, not only from boyfriends and husbands, but from members of their own family—brothers, uncles, and even fathers. I was shocked to hear of their pain and grief. Some of them had fled in such a hurry from their abusers that they had left even their children behind. Then the Social Services would come along and place those children into temporary care. Well, I knew what that was like, so I shared my story with them.

I wanted to give these women hope, but how could I when I did not have hope in my own life? I reminded myself that Jesus has promised anyone who believes in him a better life after death. I shared what little I did know, telling them that there would be a light at the end of their darkness if only they believed. These days any form of abuse is treated with zero tolerance, and I thank God for the prayers and petitions of people who wanted to see justice in our nation. Listening to these women's shattered, battered lives made me reflect on my own.

My husband was not a monster, it was the alcohol that was, but the abusive behaviour when he was drunk was not acceptable, so I decided not to go back to our home until he sought professional guidance. He agreed to such a promise because he wanted his children back. In my ignorance, I believed him. My husband started going to Alcoholics Anonymous, and I attended Al-Anon for the relatives of an alcoholic. There were a thousand and one things I would rather have done than attend that meeting, but I did it to save our marriage. We would sit round in a group, taking it in turns to talk. When it was my turn, I wanted to run and hide as my shyness had always prevented me from explaining myself properly. Words would come out all wrong. Although at the women's refuge I had managed okay, for some reason talking about Jesus made me feel good inside.

As husband and wife, we carried on as best we could, thinking the meetings and counselling would make the pain of our suffering go away. However, he started being a 'secret drinker' hiding bottles of drink in the most unusual places. One day, I noticed our large indoor plant was bone dry so gave it some water. As I went to do this it fell over, revealing small vodka bottles in its base! I hurriedly put them back and decided not to water the poor plant. The sad truth is my husband could never have carried out his promises to me without Jesus in his life, and neither of us were living the life that God wanted for us. Those poor boys had no stability or security in their young lives, and no solid role models to follow. *If only* we had held hands and prayed together to a great God who was waiting in the wings of our lives to help us, but we did not. That great God would have taken centre stage and things would have been different. God has given us all free will. He did not create us as puppets. If we believe in his existence and turn towards him, then goodness and mercy shall follow us all the days of our lives. *Mercy: compassion, kindness.* Following our own free will and doing things 'my way' will prove to be a difficult and uncertain life. God loved this world so much and could see we were all going aimlessly around with no sense of direction or real purpose. Some of us were messing up (me, big time!) so God decided to send his son, Jesus, to our world in order to help us and save us from self-destruction. That is why we have need for a saviour, 'For God loved the world so much that he gave His only Son, so that whoever believes in Him will not perish, but have eternal life,' (John 3:16). I had no idea that God had a bigger picture for my life while on this earth. I used to believe it was only *after* I was in heaven that my life would be complete. Somebody, somewhere, once quoted this phrase: 'BIBLE: Believer's Instructions Before Leaving Earth.'

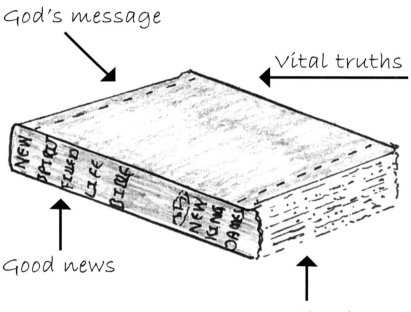

God's message

Vital truths

Good news

Instruction book

Chapter Five
Good News—Bad News

I was oblivious to God's vital truths for us as a family, so I carried on living a life under the shadow of lies. The boys made it bearable and the journey less tedious. Then another hurdle entered my life. I started experiencing bouts of extreme tiredness, which developed into something more serious. One day I just keeled over and apparently fainted. The next thing I remember was waking up in a hospital bed surrounded by student doctors!

I had various tests done at the hospital, including a lumber puncture and four blood transfusions. The diagnosis was bacterial meningitis and I remained in a feverish state for almost three weeks. My memories of my time in that hospital are still very vague, but thanks to a praying church, I made a full recovery. However, further tests revealed I was pregnant, much to my surprise, so I had to stay another week while they did extensive examinations to ensure the baby in my womb was thriving. The church continued to pray. Good news, the baby was doing well! Seven months later, I gave birth to a very healthy, beautiful baby boy. Our two boys, then aged three and four, were so excited they were getting a little baby brother!

Friends rallied round to support us; we were now a family of five. I was still weak after my illness, but I was determined to breastfeed my baby. I had done the same with my other two when they were born, it was important to me that they got this natural nourishment. If

I could give my babies nothing else, I wanted to give them a good start in this life. The church folk were very kind and supportive and helped with shopping and cleaning. I struck up a friendship with two of the ladies, and as time went on began to trust them. One day I poured my heart out to them, sharing my fears about my husband. From that day, they continued to give me moral support. They shared how much God loved me and how he wanted to be my friend, as they were. I found it hard to relate to God as a friend back then; he was more like a distant relative one would call on if in need. I never prayed or talked with him, all I did was bawl my eyes out to him every time I had a problem (which was most of the time!). I liked it when those ladies came round for chats. We received visits from the Social Services every week too, but these were not friendly little chats, but questions and concerns for my health and the boys' safety. I felt I was being put on trial at the time, but looking back now and seeing everything in perspective, I realise they were genuinely concerned for our welfare. After having my third child there was never a dull moment in our household! A baby and two young boys filled our waking (and sleeping!) hours. I was gradually getting my strength back, but it was not easy. The marriage was still very fragile, although the children gave us hope and a purpose to stay together. We loved them so very much. With the birth of each child a respite of calm was brought into our lives. Having the responsibility of attending to their everyday needs made me less self-centred. Fun and laughter entered my life in the form of cartoons, nursery rhymes and Rupert Bear! The boys happily played together and adored their baby brother. Months flew by and the journey started to look promising until a bump in the road threw me off course. Both my husband and I had stopped having counselling and attending meetings because we thought we were now managing better. I knew my husband was still secretly drinking, but his abusive behaviour had stopped; or so I had thought. What he had done was transfer his frustrations from me to his sons. At first, I was blind to what was happening, but as soon as I found out, I packed some black bin sacks with the boy's clothes and toys while he was asleep. Then I rushed to the corner shop and got them to phone the police. As usual, the police sat outside in their car while I bundled my precious brood into the backseat. My husband awoke to all the activity and began ranting and raving. When the police witnessed his behaviour towards me, they *did* intervene. I never set foot in that house again. It was probably for the best as friends told me later that my husband had gone berserk and damaged everything. He so desperately needed help and support for his serious issues, but I was not the one who could help him. I had a duty to protect our boys. We did not go to a women's refuge this time, but to a bed and breakfast hostel. We had two single beds between us and could not eat in the room, but it was clean and *safe*. The social worker explained they were treating us as homeless and I would have to report to the housing office every day until suitable accommodation came along. The bank was in the process of repossessing our family home due to the fact that the mortgage payments had not been kept up (this came as a big shock to me, as my husband never admitted to what he did with the money). There was nowhere to go and no money left, so I had no choice but to apply for a council house. I had no option but to wait in that council office every day. I would sit with the baby in my arms and the two boys playing at my feet, usually with their Star Wars figures. They reminded me of how I used to play when I was little, pretending to be a character from a book or film. Thankfully, Luke Skywalker and Hans Solo kept them from noticing their bleak surroundings! My baby, too, always appeared happy, contented and oblivious to what was going on around him. All three of them gave me hope to carry on, but they deserved better than what I could give them. Guilt grew inside me like bindweed and unforgiveness clung to me like ivy. The church we had been attending at that time was not as encouraging as I had hoped. They took a dim view of me leaving my husband and counselled us to get back together. We lived apart while we had counselling, this went on for almost a year. Meanwhile, a council house became available. It was on a council estate in an area I was not familiar with, but I was so grateful to move out of hostels and B&Bs. God was still responding to my cries for help despite me not living the life he wanted for me. He was still waiting in the wings of my life, waiting for me to respond to him.

It was a very cold winter when the boys and I moved into that house, and there was fresh crisp snow covering the large back garden; as soon as the boys saw this, their squeals of delight caused a flock of birds sheltering in nearby trees to fly away! It was a joy to see their little faces light up as they raced around the garden making footprints in the snow. There was more space indoors compared to our previous house, although the toilet was downstairs and the bathroom was upstairs. This did not concern me, but not having central heating did. The only source of warmth was a gas fire in the living room, and this would be the room in which we would eat, sleep and live for the following months. I did not possess a cooker, beds or any kitchen appliances as I had left them behind when I fled the matrimonial home. Apparently, my husband had damaged a lot of it during one of his drunken rages. I heard I was eligible to apply for grants, but this was another waiting game. While waiting, bedtime consisted of sleeping on the living room floor in sleeping bags. The boys thought this great fun! We continued the camping theme with folding table, chairs and a gas camping stove. By late spring, we had collected the basic essentials so I was able to make it into a home rather than a house .However, the garden was like a jungle but there was no way I would tackle it as I hated gardening!

My eldest boy was due to start primary school and the elders of our church felt it would be better for him if my husband and I got back together (that year apart had flown by.) During that trial separation we had been encouraged to see each other a couple of times a week but live apart. I realised I still had feelings for him, but was it love? When we saw one another, he displayed affection and showered me with gifts, but was it love? My emotions were so mixed up I could not think straight, but the boys made up my mind for me. They loved their dad and wanted him back; they had enjoyed his visits and the presents he gave them, so that was it, my husband was coming home. My husband had managed to keep his job, so the benefits I had been receiving from the government had to go. The boys were still very young so I stayed at home, doing dressmaking to supplement our income. The respite of calm remained for several months until my husband's mother died. She was in hospital in a coma, and remained on a life support machine for a short time. He was beside himself with grief for months to follow. Apparently, they had had a row a few days before she became ill, and had not spoken to one another again. I could relate to his pain, it is so hard losing our loved ones. Sadly, he refused my support and sympathy. He began pushing me away, and I sensed he believed I was the source of his problem. The garage became his refuge, and I never dared go near the place. What could I do? The journey got complicated and was about to get even worse. *If only* I had turned to God and trusted him for my family, but I did not.

I discovered I was expecting my fourth child by accident. I was at the doctor's surgery waiting for blood test results when given the news. My first reaction was not a good one. I was just beginning to get my health back, 'enough is enough,' I thought. My three boys meant the world to me, but I did not want another baby, so in desperation I attempted to get rid of it. I did the most stupid things like drinking excess amounts of castor oil, strenuous exercises, and even tried falling down the stairs. I know it does not make sense to the average person, but I was so desperate, I was not thinking clearly and I did not value that life in my womb. I kept the pregnancy a secret for as long as I could, even my dear friends had no idea what I was going through. I was in a place called despair, and it was a very cold, dark and lonely place to be; but no matter how hard I tried to lose that baby in my womb, the bump kept growing month by month. When my husband found out he was thrilled, he seemed to expect me to produce a football team for him! I was aching with guilt and shame for what I had tried to do. I never told a living soul, but God knew. He was there watching me, loving me, waiting for me. He was waiting for me to cry out to him as I had done so many times before. Not this time though, as I could not face God. My guilt kept me from him, but God never left me. He just continued waiting for contact from me, and kept that flicker of hope burning in my heart and would not let it go out. What an amazing God! (I had no idea of this at the time.)

Can you identify with some or all of the issues I have mentioned in this and previous chapters? Are you in that place of despair where 'enough is enough?'

My fourth baby was born one very cold January morning, three weeks early. The nurse gave me this tiny little body to hold and the tears just streamed down my face. My mind pressed playback, reminding me how cruel a mother I was to try to abort my own baby. I was so sorry and loved that precious child from the moment he was born. He was incredibly small and did not make a sound. He did not respond to certain tests and this caused alarm bells to ring, 'Help, what have I done?'

They let me take him home before the results were due back, which surprised me. The three boys peered into the cradle

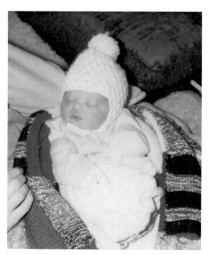

'He is so tiny!'

exclaiming 'He's so tiny!' And 'He looks like a doll!' The next day, our local GP called round to see our new arrival. I told her that the baby had slept through the night (do newborn babies do that?) and was reluctant to feed from me. That was the reason she had visited us, to tell us what the tests had revealed. Our baby had Down's syndrome, a condition caused by an extra chromosome (not due to castor oil or over exertion, much to my relief.) Hearing this news did not change a thing for me, he was still a beautiful baby that would be loved and cared for like my other sons, but my husband took a different view and went to the library to find out as much as he could about Down's syndrome. He came back armed with so many books, and kept reading aloud to me. The books were very outdated, giving negative information. He became obsessed with it, and started struggling with the fact that his son was 'different'. He believed God was punishing him for his past actions. This was so untrue, as God does not operate like that. Things escalated out of control, and fourteen months later, I made a decision to terminate our marriage for good. I did not contact the church or phone a friend this time, because I knew they would influence me. I collected my boys from nursery and school and went to the local solicitors insisting they help me there and then! A strength and determination came over me that I had never encountered before. There was no going back. Plans for divorce commenced, but the church frowned on my actions, so I had to leave. This was a blow, as I was hoping they would have supported me throughout the ordeal. The elders of the church set up meetings for me to attend, but after each session they made me feel ashamed at what I had done. I wore unforgiveness like a gown and guilt like a crown.

I was a victim of circumstances, not all of them caused by myself, but some of which I had been partly responsible for. The church did not explain the goodness of God to me. They never shared with me the love and mercy of a father God's heart toward his broken child. They chose to remind me of my faults and failings. This caused me much heartache, and shame joined the rest of my baggage that day. The best things to came out of that marriage were our four wonderful sons. I really believe in my heart of hearts that my husband loved those boys. Sadly, alcoholism can be a very hostile illness, preventing the sufferer from getting the help they most desperately need. He lived in denial, which is, of course, part of the illness. Sometimes we have to make decisions in life and take responsibility for our actions. Alcoholics find this difficult to do because their judgement is impaired and their thinking distorted; the stresses and strains of everyday living become too much for them. Not long after the divorce, my husband left the country and none of us have seen or heard from him since. The boys did not seem to be concerned about this when they were young. It was not until their teens that it became an issue.

I can only hope and pray that, wherever he is, he has found true peace and freedom from his issues as I have done with mine.

My precious brood.

Chapter Six
New Beginnings

While waiting for the divorce to be finalised I was able to take the children back to our home, as my husband had moved out. Tibby, our faithful tabby cat was still there. We gave her lots of fuss as she had been through so much herself. If Tibby could have talked, what a story she would have told! After the divorce, I stayed away from churches for a few years and God became my 'sounding board'. I was always grumbling and mumbling to him, always going to him with my moans and groans. Never taking the time to be still and listen to him, how one-sided it was. Looking back now, I think God was pretty cool to put up with my endless complaining!

Are you in this place? Do you use God as a sounding board?

The boys settled well at school, and made many friends. My time was taken up with social workers, physiotherapists, health visitors, speech and language therapists, you name them, they came! In his early years, my youngest son needed constant care and attention. He could neither walk nor talk properly until he was almost five, but he was a lively fellow and could mimic sounds and tunes. He suffered badly with eczema and was covered head to toe with it, but it did not seem to bother him. The boys adored their little brother and were very protective over him. Folk came round with lots of advice on how to bring my boys up now I was a single parent; some I welcomed with open arms; but *not* all. Some Christian friends brought me books to read which contained strange statements such as God had *chosen* me to look after my disabled child, or that God was *testing* me through my disabled child, or that my child was *extra special* and sent by God. Some books even said my son was an angel! For the sake of the reader, I want to explain that *none* of those statements are true, and will explain in a later chapter why. However, back then it suited my lifestyle to think I was 'chosen'.

Despite being free from a controlling relationship, I felt drained and somewhat disorientated. The painful divorce had left me feeling very fragile, and God, with his amazing mercy knew I needed help, so he sent this help in the form of two wonderful people. There was a knock at the door one day, and I opened it to see a smiling, jovial couple with hands outstretched to greet me! A friend had sent them with offers of help to babysit, as I needed somebody to look after my boys while I went shopping or to the dentist. This fun-loving couple may have been twenty years older, but they also had twenty years more experience than me. I could see from day one they had a deep relationship with God that I had not yet encountered. This couple were excellent with my children and became my spiritual parents for a number of years to come. God brought them into my life at a time when I most needed them and for the purpose of strengthening and establishing my role as a single mother. Their favourite saying was, 'We have come to show you how to stand on your own two feet. One day you will, and one day we will let go of your reins and watch you run—run with Jesus!'

I did eventually grow up, but it took many more years and many more knocks before I did. It should *not* have taken so long, but I was not a good listener. God was trying to get my attention through people, places and things. He never gave up on me. Where would I be today if he had? I wonder what mess I might still be in, would I still be alive?

Are you in a fragile place? Have you just come out of a bad relationship?

The couple who acted like spiritual parents to me for a number of years.

Even though my life's journey appeared to be getting better, I was still carrying a lot of baggage. My fears, insecurities and worries had refused to flee. I repeatedly allowed doubts to cloud my thinking, accepting all that came my way without dealing with it. Apparently, for every bad situation in our lives there is a good promise from God that confronts it. These promises are in God's message, the Bible. I decided to go back to church, and found one that was within walking distance from our home. This local church was not teaching about God's promises, but as I did not know about them either, I was none the wiser! The boys all went to Sunday school and we made new friends. We lived on a council estate, and many of the children from the estate came to church. When the long summer break came, there was no Sunday school, so those children just hung around the streets with nothing to do; I opened my home to them and held a group each week calling it 'summer school'. At first it worked really well, I would share a story from the Bible (I had to learn about the Old Testament stories myself *before* I could retell them back!) then each child would draw a character from the story. Sometimes we did little dramas and sang songs. I kept it simple (that is all I knew anyway!) and finished with squash and biscuits. My front room radiated fun and laughter, and my boys loved having so many friends round, but life has a funny way of coming along and spoiling one's fun. Another knock on the door; this time it was two welfare officer coming to tell me that I could not run a summer school because I did not have a licence or the qualifications to do so. They explained it was not wise to take children off the streets into my home. My reply to them was that the parents knew and had agreed to this, but it did not make a difference, as the officers were adamant it had to stop, so that was that. The children went back on the streets, leaving me feeling I had let them down. As I have said before, I just accepted knock backs without challenging or praying about them.

Life goes on, so I turned my attention to our garden. It so desperately required a makeover! I mumbled and grumbled to God, 'This garden is overgrown with weeds. How am I going to manage it on my own?' Do you know what I heard back? God spoke clearly into my heart that day. Not a booming from the sky voice saying, 'You shall cut thy grass,' but, instead, it was as if my conscience was speaking to me, 'Look at your hands.' So I did. 'You can turn your hands to anything if you try.' It reminded me of my mother telling us girls, 'Take the *t* away from *can't!*' I just *knew* it was God! From

Our wildlife pond.

that day on I started taking an interest in gardening, which I had previously loathed. My interest took me to the library for books on the subject. Then getting advice from friends and neighbours and buying packets of seeds. The boys took great delight in helping me. We began with sunflower seeds (very quick growing!) then progressed to vegetables. Within a few years, our garden was looking good. We even built a wildlife pond! Little did I realise at the time that there was a verse in the Bible that said, 'And let the beauty of the Lord our God be upon us, and establish the work of our hands,' (Psalm 90:17). God had established the work of my hands. He gave me the ability to do what I thought I could not. The beauty of the Lord was on display in our garden!

There was a big old tree in our back garden and the boys made a tree house in it. I would not let them build it too high for fear of them falling out of it, so they made it so close to the ground

that even my youngest boy could climb into it! I loved the primary school years with my sons as they were our best times together. I made every effort to give my sons a good quality of life. Money was limited (but no debt!) though we had great adventures: day trips, holidays, camping in the garden (no bogeymen here!) We would walk miles, with my youngest boy still in the pushchair, to find a beauty spot and then stop for a picnic. The older three would find a tree to climb or a stream to wade in. Life was simple but safe. My journey progressed around my sons.

Wading in the stream.

Reuben gets into the tree house
assisted by his brother. This was before
his operations.

Reuben's brothers on an adventure.

Chapter Seven
Growth

The next hurdle on my journey came in the form of a nasty virus I could not shake off. I had been suffering with a sore throat for some time, but with four energetic youngsters to care for I had no time to sit and rest! The boys were excited because we were going to a Butlins holiday. 'There is no way I can disappoint them,' I thought. We all piled into a friend's car and off we went to the seaside, with me coughing and bleary-eyed in the front seat! The first few days were okay, it was great to see the boys so happy and enjoying themselves; but from the Wednesday onwards, my symptoms got worse. I managed to take the boys to each of their activities and leave them there (properly supervised by the trained staff). When I got back to our chalet, I crashed out on the bed. The rest of the week was a similar story, the boys knew I was not feeling well, but I put on that famous brave face for their sake.

Once we arrived home, I called the doctor. My body ached so much and the headaches were *too* much. Apparently it was a virus, but when it lingered on and on blood tests were taken to find the cause. My doctor revealed that it might be M.E. (myalgic encephalomyelitis), which is commonly known as chronic fatigue syndrome these days, and is a condition causing persistent exhaustion effecting your everyday life. I was going to be sent for further tests at the hospital, and meanwhile I was to cope as best I could. Friends helped me out, but I could not stay housebound forever. My youngest was still in his pushchair so I would prop myself against it when I went out. Did this look like the abundant life that Jesus had promised us? Was I experiencing this promised life? No! Why? Because I was ignorant of these promises and did not know they even existed. Remember when

I told you I called out to God in sheer desperation in that hospital chapel? I cried out to God to save my firstborn. Then God reached down and touched my womb, and my baby was safe! God heard and answered my cry for help before I became a Christian. After I became a Christian, I would cry out to God sometimes, and every time he answered me, but what about the other times when life appeared hopeless and despair ruled me? I did *not* cry out to God. In the Old Testament of the Bible in Jeremiah 29:11–12 it says, 'For I know the thoughts that I think toward you, says the Lord, thoughts of peace and not of evil, to give you a future and a hope. Then you will call upon Me and go and pray to Me, and I will listen to you.' Isn't that wonderful? I called to God and he *did* listen to me! Jeremiah 29:13 goes on to say, 'And you will seek Me and find Me, when you search for Me with all your heart.' This is what I did *not* do. I did not search for God with all of my heart.

Here I was again crying to God, having a pity party! 'I am not well, how am I going to look after my sons?' He answered me two days later. A friend whom I had lost touch with felt led to pay me a visit. When she arrived, I was huddled in the armchair with a hot water bottle and blanket. After she left, it was as if a breath of fresh air had swept through my home. Before leaving she invited us to her church the following Sunday. I was not keen, but accepted as I did not want to hurt her feelings—she was so kind to me.

The night before we were due to go to my friend's church, I woke up in absolute agony. My shoulder blades felt like they were on fire. I tried to get out of bed but could not stand up straight, so spent the rest of the night sitting in the armchair. It was a struggle to get the boys and myself ready for church the next day, but I did it! My friend sent a very kind man to collect us, though he was quite shocked when he saw my lively brood rush towards his car! He was soon reassured that we were not hooligans, and has since become a very good friend.

The church was in a conference room of a hotel, and when we walked in, there was beautiful music playing which made me feel at ease. Much of what the pastor said was way above my head, he obviously presumed we all knew our Bibles! Although, in fairness to him, I should have known its contents, but still had not made time to study it. At the end of the meeting, the pastor called folk to go to the front for prayer and healing. This is when I wanted to make a sharp exit! I broke out into a cold sweat and was very nervous, 'Whatever is the matter with me?' I thought. The pastor repeated his request, 'There is somebody here with pain in their neck and shoulders.'

Help! I knew that request was for me, so I sheepishly left my seat and made my way to the front for prayer. The pastor asked me if I knew Jesus as my Saviour and Lord. I said yes without hesitating. The pastor's next question was, 'Do you know that Jesus is our healer and wants to heal us of every pain?' This time I did hesitate. It surprised me, as I did not realise *every* pain could be healed. I knew of people that had been healed of their sickness and pain, but also knew many that had not. I just thought sickness and suffering were a part of life and something we had to put up with; nobody before that day had explained to me that salvation (this is when we ask Jesus into our lives) included healing. *Salvation: saving, rescue, deliverance, redemption.* To me it meant being saved or brought from an inferior existence to a better one. Apparently, Jesus had not only died on the cross on behalf of the entire human race so that we could have a better life, but he had also died so we could have healing in both body and mind! Wow! It sounded too good to be true, but it was true! A miracle was happening to me—I was free from the severe pain in my body, I could stand up straight and walk with no aches or pains! *Miracle: incredible, extraordinary, a supernatural event.* It is an amazing experience to be healed instantly of something that has been controlling one's life. To have a debilitating illness one day, and be free of it the next is hard to understand, but that is exactly what happened to me. I did not have to undergo further tests after that day! I started thinking that if I could be healed, then what about my son, diagnosed with a condition, a disability that would prevent him from living a full life like his brothers? How dare it invade my precious little boy, I thought. I want him healed too. It is beyond human comprehension to understand this; back then my heart wanted to believe, but my mind questioned it, but wanting to believe is a good place to start, and this is called hope. Hope is the step above despair, but the step below faith.

Faith: the realisation that it has happened, an assurance. This is the place to stay!

Hope: wanting something to change, an expectation of things. This is the place to start.

Despair: hopelessness, nothing, the end of your tether. This is the place to leave!

Receiving a miracle in my body inspired me to get serious with God and open my Bible. I was still a beginner in the school of truth and still carrying my 'baggage' of stuff, but at least I had begun. At last the book was opened!

There is only one God, who is the creator of our universe. Jesus Christ is God's son. Jesus lived, died and rose again for us, the world. Believing this statement is true will open up an entire new way of living to us. It will gain us entry into a love that is far above or beyond all we could ever imagine. For those who do not yet believe, God is waiting to give you this love, but until you believe and then receive this love, it will remain where it is. How do we know that God loves us? He gave us his only son to die and bleed to death for you and me. It took me a long time to understand why somebody would love me enough to die for me in order to give me a better life and a purpose for my existence. In the New Testament in Romans 5:8 it says, 'But God demonstrates His own love toward us, in that while we were still sinners, Christ died for us.'

'Sinner? Me?' Nobody likes the word *sinner*. Most people like to think they are good, and look upon the acts of sin as murder, rape, fraud, theft, etc. All of those things are not acceptable in our society, but what about lying, cheating, gossiping, judging one another, not forgiving others? (This was what I was doing). However, it is impossible to live a life free of all of those things on our own. I thought I could deal with or learn to live with my issues, but I was *so* wrong. Those nice friendly folk who have no moral code or standards to live to but their own, where do they fit into this picture? They believe they are decent people who are not doing anything wrong, and believe their standard of living will gain them entry into heaven when they die. I was the opposite, as I did not think I was good enough to go to heaven. Yet we were both wrong! Living a life by our own efforts (good and bad) causes us all to be sinners. Our moral actions become biased. Our own self-efforts, acts of kindness, doing things our own way are not sufficient without Jesus at the centre of our lives. Denying Jesus' existence and his love for us all is the greatest sin of all. We cannot earn the favour or love of God. It is a gift. All he wants from us is to believe in him then turn towards him and receive his gift of grace. *Grace: favour, goodness, blessing*; an unexpected but very welcome gift! God's grace towards us is unconditional and overwhelming. We cannot earn it, we do not deserve it, and it is free. Imagine a house where somebody has left a parcel on the front doorstep. They leave the parcel with a note attached. The owner of the house comes home and reads the note:

This is for you. Everything inside this parcel will free you from your existing life and give you hope, freedom and lasting peace in your new life. It is free. I do not want payment as I paid for it myself. It is a gift from me. I have not given it to you depending on how good or bad you have been in your life. This gift represents the life I have longed for you to live. You do not know me, but I have always known you. I have always loved you. To receive my love for you, please accept my gift.

The homeowner has two choices: accept or reject their free gift.

In my case I believed in God and his son, Jesus, but I had not made a real commitment. I had received the gift, but not opened it up! Somebody once said, 'You may have opened your front door to God, but do not leave him in the hallway; bring him into your living room and let him stay!' This is what I was doing, placing God in a corner of my life. Even after I was healed, I did not fully appreciate what Jesus had gone through to heal me.

Jesus does not want to be a part of your life, but *all* of it. Are you willing to let him?

Are you ready to accept God's gift of grace into your life?

Unbeknown to me, that hope-seed God had planted in my heart was getting stronger as I started to read his message, the Bible. The boys and I started going to my friend's church. Life appeared more settled. I had never been one for adventure before, but one day I said to the boys, 'Let's go to Cornwall for two weeks!' It is true what they say about Cornwall; all sun, sea and surfing. The three older boys loved riding the waves on their surfboards, whilst my youngest sat on the beach in wonder of it all. In reality he was old enough to join his brothers, but confined in his own world he was not able to. I looked at his sweet, chubby face and said, 'One day you will be out there, my son.' He may not have been able to ride the waves, but he had found his voice and loved singing! He had echolalia, which means everything the person hears they will repeat; so

Reuben sits on the beach while his brothers go surfing in Cornwall.

I taught him the same songs and rhymes over and over again in the hope that one day he would sing and say them independently (as he did years later, much to the surprise of some professionals who said he may never speak.) During our stay in Cornwall, we visited one of those theme parks with lots of thrilling rides, my boys enjoyed their time there, but all too soon it was time to leave. We had to rush to get the last bus back to our holiday home. The theme park was off the beaten track down a country lane, and as we headed towards the end of the lane that bus just sped past us. We all shouted and waved our hands in the air to attract the driver's attention, but it was of no use. Then we rushed back to the park to find a telephone box, but it was too late as it was all locked up! What would you have done in my situation? Mobile phones were unheard of in those days. If one were outdoors, the only source of contact would be via the red telephone box. That is, if one could find one! When all else failed I did what I should have done in the first place—prayed. I asked God to bring a taxi or even another bus along that country road. Hope rose inside of me to pray, this time I was not crying or grumbling as I used to. All five of us huddled together at the bus stop. It was teatime and the boys were getting hungry, my youngest was asleep in his pushchair. Then, all of a sudden, we heard rustling in the high bushes behind us, the boys got scared and

I tried to reassure them (although I was secretly as anxious as they were!) Those bushes opened up to reveal two tall men! They said they were concerned when they had heard children's voices, so they broke down the hedge to find out what was going on. Behind that hedge was a repair workshop, and guess what they were repairing? Fairground equipment! The men looked puzzled, wondering why we were stranded in the back of beyond, so I relayed to them our tale of woe! They invited us to their workshop, but my sons needed no invitation when they saw such an amazing sight! Some of the equipment was working, so the men let them have free rides while I had a cup of tea! They even gave us a lift home in their lorry. This was an unusual answer to prayer, but a very welcome one!

Chapter Eight
A Bump in the Road

Life remained steady for a while, that is until our darling Tibby passed away. She had been such a faithful, loving cat, we all missed her so much. I was beside myself with grief, so I asked our kind neighbour to bury Tibby in our back garden. He was a minister at his church and offered to do a little service for the boys, which I thought was sweet of him. The boys picked flowers and put them on Tibby's grave, and our neighbour said a few words. I thanked God for all the joy Tibby had given us. The boys were upset for weeks to come as they had grown up with her, and now she was gone the house seemed empty. Friends said, 'Get another one,' as if she were some item to be replaced. Tibby had been a member of our family and had stayed by my side through thick and thin, another cat could never take her place. However, I did buy the boys a hamster each, complete with fancy cages, wheels and balls! Within a few months terrapins and stick insects were added to their pet's corner.

We were not well off, but never lacked a thing, though not due to my clever budgeting this time, but due to a continual flow of God's blessings to our home. Sometimes I only had ten pounds left after paying bills, but it seemed to stretch to feed a family of five for the week. The gas company would send us a cheque saying they had miscalculated our bill. I would go to the local shop and almost every item on my grocery list was on offer! Other times I would find money on our mat posted through the door. Sometimes God prompts folk to help others—a sort of 'secret Santa' because you never find out who those folk are. God knows, and he rewards them. The Bible tells us to let our giving be in secret, and we should have a cheerful attitude towards it. When I had a need I would go to God, saying 'I only have x number of pounds to buy trainers for my boys, please let it be enough,' And it always was, and still is to this day. These blessings are for everyone if they would only believe!

I longed for my youngest son, Reuben, to go to a mainstream school. During the 1980s, only a select few disabled children were given the opportunity to get into mainstream education, but it did open the door for future developments in the area of inclusion. The Education Act 1981 abolished labels that treated individuals as inferior; names like 'backward', 'maladjusted' and 'spastic' became offensive to use. My lovely sister was taunted and teased by other children when she was a child. Even the label the doctor gave her was disgraceful—'mentally sub-normal'. Yet she is the sweetest, kindest person one could ever meet, so again I thank God for answering the prayers and petitions of our nation! Down's syndrome replaced 'mongolism'. Apparently, somebody named Mr Downs was doing research and he thought they resembled the people of Mongolia, hence the original name was born. This did not go down well with the beautiful people of that country, so out it went. There is nothing wrong with labels if they do not restrict one's lifestyle, but if they cause one to be treated as inferior or with disrespect, then they must go.

I have no objection to my son's looks. Reuben lights up a room with his smile, and has an amazing effect on everyone he meets. When he is in a 'hug and cuddle mood' he transfers a warmth that is to be treasured (I call them huggles!). What I *do* have an objection to is the limitation on my son's life caused by one extra chromosome. There are different levels of Down's syndrome, as there are of autism. Many live a full, rewarding life: work, stay healthy, even get married and have children. This is all I wanted for my son. After much prayer, he was one of those select few to get into a mainstream school. There was much opposition to begin with, but with the help of a faithful group of people, we did it!

Reuben enjoying a drumming session
at Ashton Court.

Reuben's first day at primary school.

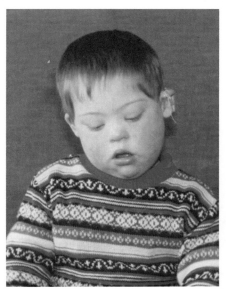

Reuben wearing hearing aids in both ears

My sister, a very precious lady to
know.

Reuben attended two schools during his primary years, the second being the most favourable. The idea was for him to mix with other children that did not have complex issues. The term used was 'to integrate with their mainstream peers'. This reminded me of the film *Born Free* where a lion cub was reared in captivity then released into the wild. Watching all those children with my son made me wonder who were wild and who were free! In the infant class, the little girls screamed and giggled, while the boys imitated animal sounds and picked their noses! 'This is a good start!' I thought, as I sat at the back of the class watching my son's every move, watching to see if he did or said anything out of place. After witnessing the other little darling's antics, I was able to relax!

At that time, Reuben suffered some slight hearing loss in both ears, so had to wear hearing aids. This he did not like and it was a problem to get him to keep them on. A group of us at church got together and prayed for total restoration of his hearing in both ears. Later that same year, the results came back from the hospital that he had normal hearing! What an awesome God we have! Reuben progressed reasonably well at school with funding for two days a week; I helped when I could, but sensed that the teachers did not like a parent's presence in the classroom. Although he could not read or write, he made up for it with his lively, loving nature. He was always full of fun and loved music and dancing. Then life brought a nasty blow to our door, knocking us right off course.

One day the school nurse wanted to have a word with me about Reuben. She was concerned that his knees would involuntarily pop in and out of their sockets. I explained to her that he was

double-jointed and was able to do amazing contortions with his body. 'You should see his crab-walk!' I told her. She was not amused and felt Reuben should see his doctor, I did not take the matter seriously and I ignored her advice. Reuben seemed fine in himself, so I thought she was overreacting.

The following week I took my two youngest boys to a bonfire night display at Castle Park. They were very excited as we sat on the bus going towards the centre of Bristol. Reuben had been walking for a few years so we had no need of a pushchair anymore. The event was grand! The firework display was tremendous; we found an excellent spot to sit and watch it all whilst tucking into hotdogs and toffee apples (the usual junk food people eat at such events!). Halfway through the evening the crowd swelled to capacity, causing me to lose Reuben. One minute he was by my side, the next he was gone. Many parents or guardians pray they will never experience such an ordeal with their children; now it was happening to me. Where could he be? It was very difficult to see as it was dark and people were jostling and pushing one another to get a better view of the display. I constantly called out his name whilst firmly holding onto my other son. I did not want to lose him too. Panic set in and I could feel my heart beating very fast. I began asking the crowd for help, and many of them were very kind and joined in the search with me. Others pretended they could not hear me, and continued their enjoyment of the event. Suddenly, screams could be heard in the distance and somebody said to me, 'Is that your child's voice?'

I immediately replied, 'Oh no, that is not my son.' I did not recognise the sound of his voice, probably because he had always been so gentle-natured and had never screamed before. Sadly it *was* Reuben who was in distress that evening. I found him lying on the ground surrounded by folk trying to help him. Reuben would not let anyone near him, he lay there having what looked like a seizure. I attempted to comfort him, but he did not seem to recognise me. It shocked me as I had never seen my son like this before. Someone shouted, 'Don't move him! The ambulance will be here soon.' I felt so inadequate as to what to do, my precious boy was lying there in pain and I could not help him. My other son was excited when he saw the ambulance drive up complete with flashing lights and the siren going!

'Mummy, mummy can I go in the ambulance, too?' He was still young and it was an adventure to him.

The paramedics struggled to get Reuben into the ambulance because he continued to scream and lash out. We were taken to A&E, with staff firing questions at me, 'Has your son had fits before? Does he suffer with epilepsy?'

My reply to their questions was, 'No, never.' I was still very shaky and bewildered as to what was happening. Reuben was sedated in order for any examination to take place, but he was not put to sleep. On examination they noticed that both of his knees were out of their sockets, concluding it was caused by the fall. As the staff proceeded to set both knees in plaster, I asked, 'Is that necessary? My son is double-jointed and pops his knees in and out all the time.'

However, they felt it was safer to put his legs into plaster casts until we saw an orthopaedic consultant. Reuben, by this time, was coming round from the sedation and pandemonium broke out! Once he saw the freshly plastered casts, Reuben ripped them from his legs in an act of frenzy, sending the white sticky stuff flying through the air in all directions—it was like a scene from a slapstick comedy! We all got covered in the stuff, folk were running for cover. A policeman happened to be in A&E at the time, and he came over to see what was going on. He attempted to speak to Reuben, but ended up with the stuff on his uniform! Reuben would not stop until every last bit was removed, then he saw me, and gave me a look that said, 'I need a hug,' so, of course, I gave him one. Reuben never cried in those days as I was told he could not produce proper tears, so he would make odd sounds. It had been a terrible ordeal for him because he had no understanding of what was going on. Screaming was his only way of communicating to us that he was upset and confused. Despite all the commotion, x-rays were taken, which revealed that nothing was broken so we all went home, much to the relief of the staff! The next day, Reuben became his friendly, loving self, and was walking as normal. However, as the chain of events which followed proved, all was not well.

We kept our appointment with the orthopaedic consultant and I was absolutely overwhelmed with what he told us. Various x-rays revealed recurring patellae dislocation and lateral subluxation. In layman's terms, for you and me, this meant Reuben's knees were 'floppy' and the ball and socket within the knees needed correction. His hips, too, were out of alignment, so a femoral osteopathy needed to be performed. They explained to me that the femur would be broken in two and a metal plate inserted to hold everything in place. It meant major surgery, but was not compulsory. The choice was mine, but they did warn me that as Reuben grew taller and heavier his bodyweight might become too much for his knees. This might cause him to fall over or not even be able to walk at all. It all seemed sudden and confusing, I could not take it all in. In that moment I lost sight of who I was and what I believed in. I was still a novice in the school of truth and had not yet learnt to take authority over the situation, because I did not know my authority! I should have gone home and thought it through, but I did not. I should have taken the time to listen to God's report about my son's health, but I did not.

I stayed and listened to the doctor's report instead. I was still undecided when I said yes to the operation, but I *did* cling to my anchor of hope.

If any of you are clinging onto hope for whatever situation you are in, please don't ever give up! Hope melts your doubts and softens your heart. It can open the door to God who has always been waiting for you, waiting for you to believe in him.

I stayed with Reuben throughout the time he spent in hospital. My eldest son was away training in the army, one stayed with a friend, and my other son was old enough to leave on his own (or so I thought, but he rang me at the hospital most evenings asking how to cook this or that!)

After the operation, Reuben was sedated on morphine and hooked up to every drip imaginable. When he came round from the anaesthetic he was extremely disoriented and anxious, and attempted to pull out his drips, catheters, dressings, etc. His distress led to aggression. Reuben started to lash out at the nurses, so he was given *more* morphine to calm him down. I wanted to cry and take his pain away from him. I felt so helpless, but tried to be brave for his sake. We kept his portable cassette recorder by his bedside with his favourite songs ready. All day and every day, I would play those songs to him. On the plus side, Reuben's reluctance to remain immobile was in his favour. He was determined to walk again, though his repeated episodes of getting out of bed and falling on the floor hindered the recovery process. We were in and out of hospital over the next few years due to infections in his wounds, mainly because he refused to keep his dressings on. A further operation took place, this time on both legs because the previous operation had not been successful. This time Reuben had plaster casts from the top of his leg to his ankle: one red and one purple! He needed a lot of aftercare when he came home. The front room resembled a hospital ward with the special bed, hoist and commode we had, so I brightened the room with balloons and banners in his favourite colours of orange and green!

Imagine going into hospital where you are put to sleep. When you wake up you cannot move your legs and are in considerable pain. Everything around you appears strange. How would you react?

Reuben reacted with outbursts of frustration leading to anger. When the plaster casts came off, he had to wear support bandages and learn to walk again with the help of a Zimmer frame. This he did not like one little bit and would send it flying across the room. As I said before, Reuben's determination to walk was admirable! He would get around by holding onto the furniture, but he hated that frame! After much physiotherapy, patience (on my part) and prayer, Reuben did eventually walk unaided around the home. However, excessive walking would aggravate his condition so the consultant advised me to use a wheelchair. The welfare team said Reuben was displaying challenging behaviour and even autism! Specialists came in and gave me a new care plan for my son's future.

'Surely the anaesthetic could have triggered off something?' I asked them. 'What about all that morphine? Is nobody listening to me?' Reuben was not the same boy that went into that operating theatre, and I felt guilty for putting him through all that. The layers of guilt within me weighed heavily on my heart. Folk kept coming round with well-meaning but *not* encouraging words. Here are the correct answers to the false information given when Reuben was born.

False: God has chosen me to look after my son and my son is 'special' sent by God.

Fact: everybody is special in the eyes of God. *All* are equal and *all* are loved. God does *not* show favouritism to anyone. In the New Testament, in Galatians 2:6 it says, 'God shows personal favouritism to no man.' I know a lot of you will want to disagree with this statement, as many of you have a beautiful child with special needs or a physical disability; but what about other children? What about the brothers or sisters of that child? Are they not as special and important? How can we differentiate between them? I have both a sister and a son with disabilities and I say from experience, *please* do not favour your child as special over the rest of the family. If we truly believe in inclusion in today's society, then let it begin in our homes. Also, how can we say we are chosen? I know some wonderful people who have never had children but are excellent foster parents to other people's. There are also some parents who have found it extremely hard to raise their disabled child, and feel guilty for giving them up. We should stop taking words like special and chosen out of context. Everybody is wonderfully made, loved and valued by God. Let us all start looking at our children and family through the eyes of God and not ourselves.

False: God is testing me through my son's disability.

Fact: God did not cause my son's condition. Neither will he use this condition to test me. God is a creator and a healer. In the New Testament in James 1:13 it says, 'Let no one say when he is tempted, I am tempted of God; for God cannot be tempted with evil, neither does He tempt anyone.' In the Old Testament in Exodus 15:26 it says, 'I am the Lord who heals you.'

God is good and everything he has created is good. Sickness, infirmity, poverty, disease and much more are products of a polluted world. It has *nothing* to do with the true God. If we let him, he can do amazing work in us and we will see the completion of this! God can change us day by day if we would *only believe*. I had very little understanding of all this when Reuben underwent his operation. I did not put my trust in God then, as I do now. I listened to negative reports about my son's health and not to God. I wanted healing for Reuben, but I did not realise it already belonged to him. I needed a revelation of this in my heart and mind. *Revelation: something revealed to somebody that previously had not been quite clear*; a penny-dropping, a light bulb moment!

Yes, I've got it now!

Chapter Nine
Dark Days

The journey got rather hectic. When Reuben arrived home from the hospital with two legs in plaster, I was his sole carer. I had to do everything for him with only an hour's respite when a care nurse called. It was a struggle at first as Reuben hated being an invalid and would not cooperate with us. However, I did admire his determination to get better, he reminded me of my mother when she was ill.

Whilst in hospital the staff presumed Reuben would wear incontinent pads throughout his stay, how wrong they were! Reuben did not like wearing them and kept asking for the toilet (the one word he *did* learn and say from an early age!) It was hospital policy that there should be no unnecessary lifting of the patients; it took two nurses to lift him onto a commode using a mechanical hoist. This did not prove popular with the nurses, as they were always busy, so they taught me how to use it. It was a great heavy thing, like a garden swing on wheels. Once Reuben was strapped in, I had to lift him up and swing him round using the correct buttons. Many a time I did it in reverse and he came flying through the air almost knocking me over, which made him chuckle. The monster even came home with us (I mean the hoist—not Reuben!). To make the hoist blend into the surroundings, I hung brightly coloured balloons and ribbons across the bar at the top. Reuben and I also played basketball over the large frame. Just because Reuben was bedbound did not mean he could not have fun! When the plaster casts came off and Reuben learnt to walk again, there were still problems with his knees. There was talk of a further operation, but this time I declined. There was no way I would put my precious son through all that again.

Reuben had to leave mainstream education and go to a school for children with learning difficulties. I asked God for guidance as to which school would most suit my son, and we found one! It had excellent facilities and Reuben settled in very well.

Even though Reuben was walking about, he got tired quickly and his knees gave way under him, so we both had to get used to the wheelchair. Reuben happily sat in it whilst I reluctantly pushed it! It was a new world to me pushing that thing. I came across so many places that were *not* wheelchair friendly. Did you know that some old buildings have preservation orders on them (due to historic interest) and so are exempt from having their doors widened to accommodate wheelchairs? There are also laws that say all public places *must* provide a ramp, but many do not; or they had a portable ramp that was so heavy it required two people to manage it. Some places I visited

Reuben outside his new school—a school for children with learning difficulties.

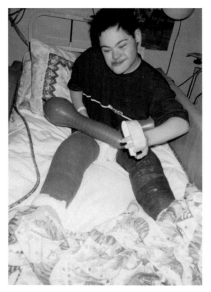

Reuben sporting two brightly coloured plaster casts. This was his last operation.

did not know where the ramp was stored! On the plus side, there were some places that welcomed us with open arms. I discovered

An overweight Reuben trying out his new wheelchair.

Playing basketball over the hoist after Reuben's last operation.

that just because somebody is in a wheelchair does not mean they cannot travel and have fun!

A few years prior to Reuben being in hospital we moved to a larger house. My sons were growing up and needed more space and privacy. The two older boys were in secondary school so each had a room of his own. The younger two shared the big main bedroom. The garden was *huge*! Good job I like gardening now, I thought! We spent many wonderful summers in that garden. The view was amazing with beautiful sunsets at night. Set on a hill in the distance was the City of Bristol College, formerly the Müller Homes.

I did not know the history of George Müller until I read a book about him. Apparently, when he was young he was into drinking and gambling, until he found Jesus (or should I say Jesus found him!) and his life completely changed. He was walking in the streets of Bristol (during the nineteenth century) and was shocked at what he saw. Children, abandoned or orphaned, living in the gutter

Our second garden with Müller Homes in the distance.

without any one to care for them. George Muller's heart was full of compassion, and he vowed to get every single child off the street. By prayer alone he was able to keep his vow, and homes were found or built to house those street kids. George Muller read God's promises in the Bible and believed them. He became a pioneer for his cause by simply trusting in the truth: the Word of God. My whole life could have changed for the better there and then if I had done the same, but I did not.

Reuben was still displaying mood swings since the operations. The aggressive outbursts continued, but not every day, thank goodness. Behaviour therapists came on the scene to show me how to deal with them. I was still convinced the anaesthetic had triggered something off in Reuben, as he was such a different boy. My other sons seemed different, too. This was not due to anaesthetic, but something far more complicated called adolescence! None of us have escaped this condition, we have all been through it or have got it to come. Prior to the 1960s, teenagers could not express their true emotions, because they were either suppressed or denied. The explosion of the fashion and music industries in the 1960s enabled the teenagers of that decade to do their 'own thing'. This was not good. It was like taking the cork off a bottle of champagne! It went from the sublime to the ridiculous and has been continuing ever since. When I was young I thought I was either mad, bad or sad as nothing was ever explained to me. I was told it was 'a phase I was going through,' so I just added adolescence to my list of hang-ups! These days society embraces, panders, excuses and feeds this hormonal package until it bursts at the seams. We did not get it right years ago and we are *still* not getting it right! My sons experienced much trauma during their early years so I wanted to create a safe and loving home for them. I wanted to be there twenty-four-seven and be their friend, nurse,

cook, carer, teacher, and, of course, their mum! I became the typical over-protective mother, and did not give my sons enough space to grow and make their own choices or mistakes in order to learn. Even though my faults were many and I was not the perfect mother (who is?) I have good memories from their childhood. Our large selection of scrapbooks and photograph albums are proof of this.

So it was no surprise that when each in turn reached adolescence, they made their voices heard! The once friendly 'if you like' became a gruff 'whatever!' Adolescence is not an easy time for either the young person going through it, or the parent/carer/relative watching from a distance. The young person has to contend with mood swings, bodily changes, facial hair and spots, around the same time as they move to the *big school*. Adjusting to new surroundings with new rules in a new body is tough. I know because I have been there.

Peer pressure, not eating properly, preoccupied with your looks; suddenly the world is not a fun place to be anymore. Most of you have been there, too.

Then all too soon it is time to go out into the big, wide world. When I was about to leave school, my dad told me, 'You have two choices, either stay on at school and study, or leave and get a job.' So I left and got a job! Then my dad said, 'Give your mother half of your wages,' so I did. Nowadays there are too many options and choices for young minds to grasp, and too much pressure for them to excel at everything. *Not* everyone is university material. Others may *not* have creative or artistic abilities. Some do not *want* to be a doctor, bus driver, or sing for their living, but some *do* and some

will. Every single person on this planet has hidden qualities, some may be aware of this, others may not. God sees these qualities in us, he values us for who we are, not what we can offer. He knows our weaknesses and can turn them into strengths. He takes the limit off our limitations! All he wants from us is to acknowledge him, believe in him, and live our lives with him. He can then guide and help us make the right choices and decisions. God makes a way when there seems to be no way.

Would you like to see your son or daughter reach their full potential without the world's pressure upon them? Only God can make this happen.

Was I going God's way when my sons reached adolescence? Did I trust God for the general health and well-being of my family? Sadly, no. I allowed the storms of life that came my way to be the dominant influence and lost direction. I looked at my circumstances instead of looking to God for answers. I had not yet learnt to trust him. *Trust: believing and depending on something or someone.*

This is what happened: my sons were growing up into handsome young men, and did not depend on me as much as they used too. They were not my babies any more. Parenting at that time became quite a challenge for me, and I started to feel redundant and helpless. The world with all its trappings, temptations and trivial pursuits was enticing my sons away from me. I could not save or protect them from the outside world. The closeness we had known for so many years departed overnight, replaced by the seeds of misunderstanding. My anchor of hope was slipping away, and the fears and insecurities stored in my mind came rushing out to overwhelm me. I loved my sons so very much, but they became strangers to me. The changes affected all of us; they reached puberty when I reached the menopause, not a good combination! However, I was their mother, the one who was supposed to keep it all together, the strong oak and solid rock. So what happened to me? Quite simply, I lost it! One morning I woke up not wanting to get out of bed, my body ached all over but my mind ached even more. I was an emotional mess and had lost the motivation to do anything. I thought my sons would be better off without me, as I found their needs too great to handle. Seeds of bitterness blew our way, and one by one, I wanted them to leave. Guilt hovered over me like a dark cloud, I went back down on that step of despair and had not the strength to move. My youngest stayed at home, but I managed to get a considerable amount of respite care to get me through those dark days.

Some of you may be thinking how irresponsible to let my offspring go. You are right, I was irresponsible, but this is what happens to a

person when they fall in to that place called despair. It is a controlling place where one loses all sense of right and wrong. If you can, try to imagine you are in a room that is suddenly plunged into darkness. You cannot see a thing, and you cannot feel your way around because you are unfamiliar with the surroundings. You find yourself locked in a prison of anxiety and fear. Despair has a foothold and throws away the key. You desperately search for this key, which is extremely difficult in total darkness. Utter exhaustion comes over you, and you wonder if you will *ever* get out of this place. For some, especially if they have been there only a short while, sheer determination to escape keeps them going; but for others who have been there a long time it can be too much to bear, and they lose the will to escape. I thank my God I was in that place for only a short term. During those dark days, I stopped praying and talking to God because I was full of guilt and shame. I felt a complete failure for not being able to keep my family together. My shame locked me in a cocoon of isolation. I did not go to church, as they were not sharing the goodness of God, but the wrath of God. Some frowned on my bouts of depression, expecting me to 'snap out of it' and 'pull myself together' without trying to understand the whole situation. If only they had walked alongside me at my pace and listened to the pain and cry of my heart. If only they had explained to me how Jesus had removed my shame and guilt for good, and wiped the slate of my life clean so I could start again. Instead, they told me to constantly confess my sins to God, then go and make a joyful noise to him! Some churches (not all) are so sin-conscious and fault-picking it must grieve God very much. In the Bible, Jesus tells us he came to our world to heal the broken hearted, and set the captive free; he also tells us to come to him if we are weary and laden down with troubles. I had yet to discover this wonderful truth, so was approaching Christianity as a work's programme and not an enjoyable adventure. However, all that was about to change! I thank God for a handful of precious friends who never gave up on me throughout those dark days; they never judged my actions or took sides. They stayed in close contact and encouraged me to get back on my journey towards hope. God himself was always there, watching and waiting for me.

Chapter Ten
A Light at the End of the Tunnel

'If only I could put the clocks back and make everything right,' is a familiar saying in most homes! We can all confess to regrets in our lives, but we must not carry them with us, we need to let go and move on. This was hard for me to do back then. My journey had come to a halt and I did not know which way to go. Then, one day, I noticed my Bible on the table. I picked it up and skimmed through it, resting on the Psalms (Old Testament.) The Psalms are like poetry in motion, expressions and declarations sharing the greatness of an awesome God! Many of the Psalms start with cries of despair turning into hope when they discover what an amazing God they have. There seemed to be a lot of crying out to God! 'I cried out to God who does everything to help me. He sends help from Heaven and saves me. He sends me His love and peace,' (Psalms 57:3). 'I asked the Lord for help and He answered me. He saved me from all that I feared,' (Psalms 34:4). God says, 'When you call to me, I will answer you. I will be with you when you are in trouble,' (Psalms 91:15).

People in the Psalms seemed to be getting in to a right old mess, but it all changed when they put their trust in God! This encouraged me and gave me comfort. For several days I read those Psalms, then I casually flipped over to Isaiah (still in the Old Testament). In chapter forty-two, verse three it says, 'A bruised reed shall He not break, and the smoking flax shall He not quench.'

It was one of those moments when the words jump out of the page and speak directly to you! It reminded me of the time when God had spoken to me through my conscience to take up gardening. It was an incredible moment as I sensed God was saying, 'You are that

bruised reed and I will not let you break.' *Conscience:
moral sense of right and wrong; a still, small voice.*
I heard the still, small voice of God that day. He
breathed life back into my whole being. How
awesome is that! I climbed up onto the step
of hope where I felt safe. I had been up and
down those steps for years, this time I
wanted to stay put!

*If you are in that place of despair I pray for a total breakthrough in
your situation and that it will come very soon.*

I started waking up to the fact that I could not manage my
life without Jesus anymore. We come to Jesus in our imperfect
state and embrace perfection. This simple act connects us to him.
We can bring to him nothing of ourselves. He does not point the
finger as the world does. He does not judge or scold us as we do
to one another. Did you know that God has your name written on
the palm of his hands? Some of you may be searching for the real
meaning to life. *Does God exist? Will the genuine God reveal himself
to me? Are you there God?* If you are sincere in what you saying, then
God will answer. He will come alongside you and make you aware
of his existence. A light comes on in your heart, and you make
the connection by saying you believe in God and his son Jesus. A
relationship begins. You have come home! This should be a life-
changing experience and not just something
we felt we should do because our friend did
it, or our parents told us to do it. The Bible
refers to it as being 'born-again'. We all come
into this world through our mother's womb
in physical birth. We usually commemorate
this event by having a birthday every year.

Jesus refers to a second birth that we can

have by believing in Him. In the New Testament, John 3:5–7, Jesus says: 'I tell you the truth; unless one is born of water and the Spirit they cannot enter God's Kingdom. Human life comes from human parents, but spiritual life comes from the spirit. Do not be surprised when I tell you, "You must be born again."' The first birth is through human contact, and the second birth is through spiritual contact. We make contact with God by being fully convinced that Jesus is real in our lives, and he alone is the son of God. Some people use the term *getting saved*. 'Saved from what?' you ask. Saved from our existing lives to a new one that lasts forever! Some of you reply, 'I am happy with the one I have, thank you very much, I don't need a new one.' As I have mentioned before, we all have a creator to help us through this life. Not recognising our creator will cause us to wander along a wide path that leads to all sorts of difficulties. Look at my life! Doing it *my way* will not last forever. Making the decision to be born again is not something to be taken lightly. It is not a game or a hobby, but a real life-changing event. Look at me, I went through the motions of being born again, but did not take it seriously or understand its meaning. I genuinely believed that Jesus was real and heaven was a place to look forward too, but did not explore my new life in him. Once I received my free ticket to heaven I continued on my journey as before. All that changed when I actually started to read the Bible. I learnt that God wants a relationship with us, not silent partners. When two people get married, they include and involve each other in everything they do. Jesus wants to do the same. Remember, being born again is a spiritual partnership *not* a human one. I had pushed God away and put him in a corner of my life and left him there, I was disconnected from a loving God who wanted me back. Think of electricity. When we unplug the kettle, the electricity is still there! The power supply has not been switched off. I pulled the plug on my contact with God, but he had not gone away from me.

If you have never known God, would you like to connect to him? If you are disconnected from him, do you not think it's about time to be reconnected?

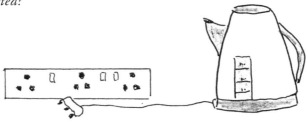

I began making progress on my journey, slowly but surely. The first and most important thing I wanted to do was to restore my relationship with my sons. It was difficult for them to keep in touch with their mother who, one minute was having a kind of breakdown, then the next minute wanted to kiss and make up! They were fine young men embarking on their own journey of life. There were scars. We all knew we could never go back to how it was, but we could go forward, so the process of forgiving one another began taking place. I realised they had grown up so we could not play happy families anymore, but we could build bridges. There are some days, even now, that I wish I could go back in time before everything went wrong between my sons and I. Losing the people so dear to you can be very painful; I lost my sons to the world and it is only through trusting in God and his amazing love that we are close again. God has shown me how much he loves them, and I draw my strength from this amazing revelation. The love Jesus has for my family is enough to repair the broken pieces of our lives. Our wounds go deep, but Jesus' love goes deeper.

Chapter Eleven
At Last!

Imagine a vehicle that only operates on positive thoughts and encouraging words. This vehicle does not stay still but travels from the present to the future. We use it a lot but do not appreciate its full potential. It picks us up from where we are and takes us to where we should be heading!

At last, I was moving in the right direction with a new strength within me. It was becoming a journey of discovery. I had reconnected with both a great God and great sons. I actually found a church that encouraged believers to find out more about the Holy Spirit (these churches do exist!). I never really appreciated the Holy Spirit's role in my life until I began attending this church. 'Who is the Holy Spirit?' you ask. Until one is born again, all this will remain a mystery! Jesus tells us he will give us a helper to understand our new life with him, 'I will ask the Father, and he will give you another Helper to be with you forever. The Helper is the Spirit of truth. The people of the world cannot accept him, because they don't see him or know him.' (John 14:16–17). The Holy Spirit is the spirit of truth sent by God through Jesus to all who believe!

The only way we can understand this stuff is through revelation, a 'light bulb' moment! The Holy Spirit's job is to reveal to us that God really does exist and the Bible is true. The Holy Spirit will make things clear to us. 'I can see clearly now, the rain has gone.' That old song says it all! This is what started happening to me. When I recognised the Holy Spirit's role in my life, it brought everything into perspective and began changing my way of thinking. One day I went to a Christian event with some friends, and heard some mind-boggling stuff! The speaker was explaining that human beings have been designed by God as a three-part being: spirit, soul and body. Wow! This is different, I thought. I had always presumed that spirit was another name for soul, and we have two parts: soul and body. Apparently, some people believe we are: mind, body and soul! So who is correct? I went to the Bible for answers, and in the New Testament, 1 Thessalonians 5:23 it says, 'We pray that God himself, the God of peace, will make you pure—belonging only to him. We pray that your whole self—spirit, soul, and body—will be kept safe and be blameless when our Lord Jesus Christ comes.' Recognising the Holy Spirit as my helper, I was able to ask him to show me this truth (yes, we can talk to the Holy Spirit! He is a spiritual being not a thing or a force, as some believe) I did further studies, and I am now absolutely convinced that human beings are exactly what the Bible says they are, a three-part being. It started to make sense to me that God originally intended for the spirit in this threesome to oversee the other two, soul and body.

Whole Self:

Spirit. The purpose of our spirit is to communicate with God. In John 4:24 it says, 'God is spirit and those who worship Him must worship in Spirit and Truth.' When we get born again our spirit wakes up and makes this connection (remember the kettle!). With our spirit the stronger of the threesome, we will have a greater sense of freedom. In 2 Corinthians 3:17 it reads, 'The Lord God is Spirit and where the Spirit of the Lord is there is liberty.' *Liberty: freedom.*

Soul. This is where our mind, will and emotions are. This is the see, hear, taste, touch, smell part of us; our five senses. It is not wise for our soul to be the stronger of the threesome. I had allowed my soul to rule me, with emotions running riot and my mind constantly reminding me of my fears and faults. My will influenced all the choices and decisions I made, and—as you have discovered—I made some bad ones! Emotions can be good and are very beautiful in their place, but if they 'get out of place' can be insensitive, immature, and destructive.

Body. This is our covering, our outer shell that houses our spirit and soul. The body responds to what the spirit and soul do. We all know that the body reacts to the mind, will and emotions. When I suffered with anxiety, my body developed many symptoms.

When I realised I had been living from a place of discomfort—my soul—and now had the opportunity to move into a place of safety—my spirit—I was over the moon! All my life I had been under the influence of negative, unhealthy thoughts: fear, worry, gossip, resentment, lies, offense, and more. They bred and festered while my soul was in charge.

Move over soul! My spirit is in charge now!

So any decisions I made, were based on the wrong information or negative instructions stored in my mind. I watched horror films and wondered why I had nightmares! I would speak unproductive words over myself and others.

Does any of this sound familiar to you? Do you go around spreading doom and gloom over yourself and others? Do you really want your mind to be the controlling influence on your life?

We all have the opportunity to turn our lives around for the better by focusing our minds on the truth. That mindset of negativity had dominated my thinking for so long; it had to go! Once I got hold of this truth, my attitude to life started to change; negatives ran out the door and positives rushed to greet me!

contentment

joy

calm

→

peace

hope

anger

hate

shyness

→

fear

phobias

I was in my late forties, and my life up until then had been a mere shadow of who I really was. The difference was that I had crossed over from unbelief to believing. From casually following Jesus to giving him full access into my life. My journey went from shades of grey to Technicolor! I found myself smiling more, developing a sense of humour, and being considerate of other people's needs. I started to appreciate so many of the things that life had to offer: birds singing (the song of the blackbird is beautiful!), glorious sunsets, the amazing change of colours that each season brings, and much more. Ordinary everyday things like hot water and heating at a turn of a dial; soft fluffy towels; duvets and pillows; food of all descriptions, tastes and smells. For so long I had taken these things for granted. God wanted to be included in the journey I was taking, and wanted to walk not behind or in front, but alongside me. When I felt frail, God saw strength; when I felt discouraged, God saw hope; when I felt a failure, God saw a winner. He was delighted I wanted to spend time with him. He was not waiting in the wings anymore, but taking centre stage!

Chapter Twelve
Step of Faith

The journey was looking promising, and I began managing things better. Even though I was aware life still would not be plain sailing, I also knew that the captain of my ship would steer me through troubled waters! Life on this earth will always throw unwelcome stuff our way; the important thing is how we handle that stuff. My track record in this area was very poor, so I am grateful to God for wiping the record clean and giving me a new life. When I was young, my mother used to say, 'Don't make a mountain out of a molehill!' Jesus tells us in Matthew 17:20 that if we have faith the size of a mustard seed we can tell the mountain to move! Both my mother and Jesus were referring to something that is getting out of control in our lives. Throughout my life I had caused many molehills to become mountains. For example, the one spider in my bedroom became an army of them. Many a night I would sleep with the light on for fear of that one spider bringing all his mates back with him! It sounds funny now, but that one small fear turned into a phobia, along with lots of others. My childhood fears were hard to shake off and grew into mountains of anxiety, worry and stress. A few weeks before writing this, I spotted one of those large garden spiders in my bedroom. I managed to get him in a jam jar and pop him outside. There was no way I could have done that years ago. Though I admit I would not like it crawling on me, I have come to realise spiders are beautiful creatures and not pests. They kill lots of nasty bugs and flies, so we should appreciate them and not fear them. The house spiders can stay in their nooks and crannies, and the garden spiders can weave happily away in my garden!

Some mountains we attract, others we do not; Jesus shows us a way round them or helps us to deal with them head on. That problem or situation in our lives has *no right* to stay and get out of control. The Bible is God's message to us all. As I have said before, we will not understand any of its contents until we are born again. If we truly believe, the Holy Spirit will open our hearts (where our spirit is!) to receive God's message. Imagine a garden with no flowers, shrubs or trees; everywhere is barren. You want to make it look nice so you buy some seeds and bury them in the ground. Those tiny seeds begin to emerge above the soil, but it rains so hard some of them get washed away. The remaining baby seedlings continue to grow, but you forget to keep an eye on them when some nasty bugs decide to eat them for their supper! The few that survive are thirsty, but you forget to water them before you leave on your month-long trip. That month is the hottest month on record, leaving the ground extremely dry. Those poor seedlings, it is a wonder that any survive! The story of my life was like this garden, the ground was my heart and God's message of love, hope and forgiveness was the seed. Jesus planted a hope seed in my heart the day I invited him into my life. At first, I did not follow his message, so the rain of this life came and washed away the hopes and promises that it brought. I fell down, but managed to get up again. The seed grew within me and started to take root. Then two horrid bugs called pain and despair caused me much heartache, so I withered and fell by the wayside. My seed remained dormant, but did not die. The seed that is planted in our hearts through believing in God and the message he brings can only die if we reject him and his teachings. Disconnection is not rejection, but if we stay distant for too long we may forget him.

I urge you to keep the hope seed in your heart watered and fed regularly by asking the Holy Spirit to show you God's promises for your life. If you do not yet believe, I urge you to call out to a God who already believes in you.

Without God, we have no hope, with God we do. I cannot emphasise enough how much my life has changed since I started trusting in God and his son, Jesus. You think you can manage without him, and can deal with your mountains? Maybe you can temporarily, but not in the long term, there can be no growth unless we are firmly rooted in the truth. In John 6:33, Jesus says, 'You can have peace with me; in this world you will have trouble, but be encouraged as I have defeated this world.'

Look around at the state our world is in, our society is crumbling. Jesus came to restore order out of chaos. Jesus gives us hope that we are not alone. Jesus is telling us, 'Take heart, hold on in there, I have got hold of you, you will be safe with me.' Are we listening? I bear witness to the fact that Jesus helps me separate my molehills and mountains, and deal with them one by one.

My hope seed eventually grew into faith as I continued to trust God, and believe in his word (his message, the Bible.)
At last I had reached the step of faith where I belonged and would keep on growing!

Faith: a strong belief, trust, an absolute assurance. One just knows in one's heart it is true!

Despair

Hope

Faith

'Yippee!'

Chapter Thirteen
Stubborn Roots Removed

My journey was getting interesting, especially with less baggage to carry round with me. My childhood fears left when I found out that God's perfect love drives out all fear. I stopped allowing my mind to rule me, and I replaced it with the peace of God who guarded my heart. I developed a genuine joy that remained with me regardless of any situation that came my way. Long-suffering is another word for patience, this virtue I did *not* have until I developed faith in God's amazing love!

My youngest son, Reuben, was living with me at the time and seemed calmer, both at home and at school. Although he was still struggling with coming to terms with his limited mobility, he was more relaxed emotionally. I think the change in me might have had something to do with it, as I was not the stressed, neurotic mum he had witnessed in the past! I may not have been able to go back in time and put everything right, but I could make up for lost time. I often spent quality days with each of my sons, visiting them and having meals together, just doing the stuff that mums (and dads!) do.

However, I still had two major issues to deal with: nobody would have known I was still carrying guilt and unforgiveness around with me. I wanted to forgive, and this is a good place to start. I sensed that Jesus was gently persuading me to give up the pain I had lived with for so many years. There was no resistance, I just wanted it to go. The breakthrough came through a break away! Close friends invited me to a Christian event in the

Midlands. Now I was off to have quality time for me! My friends and I stayed in a lovely guesthouse; we each had our own bedroom with en-suite. The breakfast was delicious, I so enjoyed being waited on! It was a three-day event, and on the second day one of the Christian speakers announced he was going to talk about unforgiveness. I felt uneasy and started thinking, 'I hope this guy does not ask people to go out for prayer.' My heart was beating fast and I wanted to go to the toilet. It was not easy to get out as I was sitting in the middle of a row with ten to fifteen people either side of me! I edged my way past them, brushing knees, kicking over bags; somebody's bottled water went rolling down the aisle. Then that person picked up a different bottle believing it was theirs, and I never said a thing. I rushed out through the wrong exit and had to come back in to go through another exit! *Can you identify with this moment?*

Instead of the speaker going through the motions of 'twenty steps towards forgiving somebody,' he calmly spent the next hour sharing how much Jesus loves us, and why Jesus died for us on that cross. Overwhelmed by what the speaker said, it moved me deeply. Tears poured down my face as I discovered how much we are all worth to Jesus. Much was revealed to me that day that I had never understood before. I started to realise that Jesus had already broken the power of my past over me. My past could no longer hold me because Jesus had dealt with it already. Jesus knew I found it difficult to forgive my abusers myself, so he took all the stuff I was carrying: guilt, shame and unforgiveness, and placed them on *himself*. Over two thousand years ago, Jesus Christ was nailed to a wooden cross and died a slow, agonising death for stuff he had *not* done. Imagine if we could weigh the whole world's weaknesses, faults, sadness, pains, sufferings, wrongdoings and much more. They would be very heavy indeed, far too heavy for anyone to carry. Yet this is *exactly* what Jesus did! The Bible says that Jesus took the whole weight of the world's sins upon himself.

'Oh no!' you say. 'She is mentioning that word again—*sin*.' You say, 'I do good and would not harm anybody, I am not a bad person and I give to charity.'

What about when we judge another's behaviour? What happens if we cause offense through the words we speak? Is it okay to ignore the smelly drunk on the street pavement? Is it fair to sign a petition to stop ex-offenders coming to live near us? Should we never forgive the train driver who fell asleep while driving a train, causing a terrible accident? Do we hate the person who stole from us for the rest of our lives? If we are honest, we will realise we cannot change the way we think, act, say or do through our own strength. Our own strengths are flawed and do not meet the standard of perfection. Only in God's strength can we achieve this perfection. God wants us to forgive, but understands it is impossible without his help. God wants us to love one another, but understands many of us will find this difficult. That is why his son made a way so we can do these things. We live in a world that has been polluted and ravaged by sin, and this affects both you and me. From the beginning of time, the pollution of sin has caused us all to lose sight of who we are and where we came from; but all is not lost because Jesus has come to help us get back on track and give us a new identity! We have to connect to God to get our identity back; *only* through Jesus can we do this.

Many of you say, 'I believe in Jesus!' but do not believe that the Bible is relevant in your day-to-day life. If a newspaper reporter went around asking people if they believed in Jesus, many people would say yes. However, if that same reporter asked the same people if they believed in the Bible, most of them would reply no! I was one of those people. I always thought there was a God, and I enjoyed watching those old Jesus films on the television. However, the Bible scared me. I went to a Church of England school from the age of eleven, and this is where an unhealthy fear of the Bible took root in me. I was not bullied by children, but by the teachers! They forced every pupil to learn each chapter and verse without explaining its meaning. Every week, each child in turn would have to stand at the front of the class and recite a passage of scripture from memory. I hated those times. My crippling shyness prevented me from speaking properly; I would stand there shaking and sweating while the rest of the class thought it great fun. The girls giggled while the boys sneered. The teacher, on the other hand, was not amused. Intimidation and ridicule ruled in the schools of the 1960s and '70s. I was always the one the teacher singled out as an example to others. My crime: forgetting Bible verses. My punishment: standing in the corridor throughout every break time, for a whole day. I spent long hours trying to memorise those verses, but each time it came out all wrong. This is an example of how our minds can keep us trapped in fear and anxiety. My mind relayed back to me the wrong picture about God and the Bible. The crazy thing was I was forced to learn out of fear, words that one day would become so dear to me. Some of you may have heard of the song of Mary, often called the Magnificat. You will find it in Luke 1:46–55. The words that Mary speaks are a beautiful expression of her heart when she realises she has been chosen to carry the Son of God in her womb! We all know the famous story of Jesus being born of a virgin named Mary in unwelcome circumstances (no room at the inn). Do we really understand it is not just a story? The Magnificat was one of several verses I had to memorise as a child, and I *hated* those words. Yet years later, these very same verses are incredibly special to me. Mary sings from her heart and recognises she has a spirit and a soul! Read it for yourself. The Bible is only hard to believe and impossible to understand until the light is switched on in our heart. We should not separate Jesus from the Bible; we cannot claim to believe in one and not the other. Sadly, the world lives in denial of this truth.

When I discovered Jesus had placed a high value on my life through his death; when the truth dawned in my heart that Jesus had dealt with my unforgiveness, I was able to close the door on painful past memories for good. He had made a way for me to be free. When I truly forgave my abusers it did not make the act of abuse acceptable, but it freed me so that the connection was not there anymore. It was like a release mechanism that unlocked the *un* from the *forgiveness*. Only Jesus can do this: he took both our suffering and punishment instead of us. He paid the price for both the abused and the abuser. He exchanged our lives for his. Resentment and guilt had worn me down, now I was free it felt like a gentle breeze flowing through my body—at last I felt clean! It is not worth holding on to the tragedies of our pasts because we keep the door open to our pain when we do not forgive. I used to present myself one of two different ways: I'd either break down under pressure and bawl my eyes out; or I'd put on a brave face with 'the show must go on' attitude. Both were denying me the freedom to live a normal, healthy life. The first one was bringing my pain to the surface but letting it play havoc with my emotions. The second one was suppressing my pain but living in denial. We should not deny the existence of our present or past trauma, *but* we do not have to live with them. The only safe way we can continue our journey in this life is to put those heavy bags down and leave them there. Jesus will pick them up and get rid of them for us; but we have to ask him first. He will not intrude without our consent as we all have free will.

This was me.   This is me now.

Are you struggling with baggage or issues that you find hard to leave behind? Can you leave them with Jesus and trust him to help you move on with your life? It is a recovery process, but you will recover. Only believe.

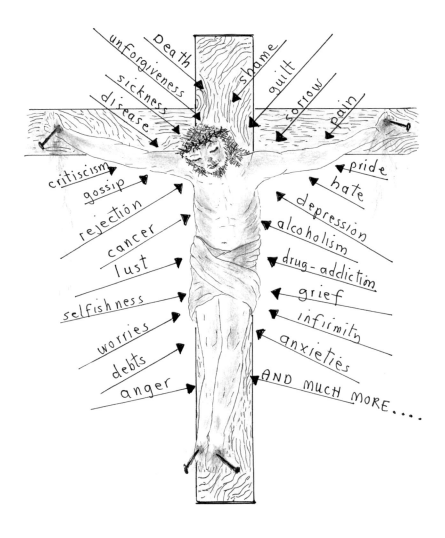

Jesus said, 'Come to Me all you who are heavy laden and I will give you rest. For My burden is light and My yoke is easy.' (John 8:36).

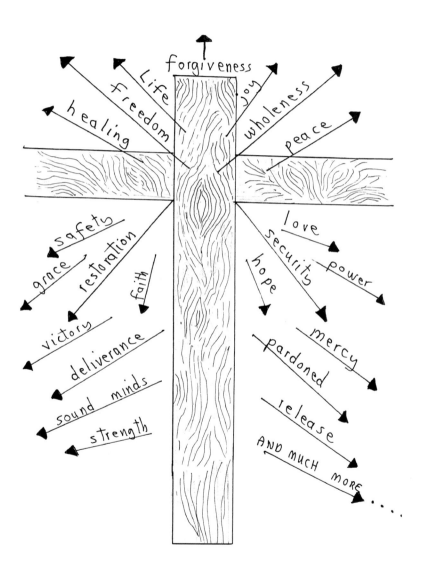

Chapter Fourteen
On the Move

After that event in the Midlands I came home a different person; so did my friends! We began studying the Bible together, and discovered a mine of information. It was like unearthing hidden treasure, the more we found, the more we wanted! The Old Testament *leads* us to Jesus and the New Testament shows us how to *live* with Jesus. With the help of the Holy Spirit, we were able to understand what had previously been a mystery to us. My journey was becoming so good I was able to relax and enjoy the view!

The house I was living in at the time was too big for us. My two eldest sons had moved away from Bristol a few years earlier, and my other son was very understanding when I told him my plans to move. I was in a rented property so I was able to go through the process of home swapping. The plan was not to move too far, just a few miles into the suburbs, but God had a different plan to mine! The idea of home swapping is to exchange your home for somebody else's; you advertise in the paper or a local register that is in the council offices. The plus side is you can view as many properties as you like, but on the minus side, your home needs to be spotless and minimalistic twenty-four-seven! I was neither house proud nor a lover of clutter, but I love colour coordinating everything (usually in shades of red!). A parade of folk came and went over the next few months who were interested in my house, but I was not interested in theirs after viewing them. The houses either looked good but the location did not, or the location was stunning but the property was not; so one day I put my hands in the air saying, 'Okay, Lord, you know best. Where do *you* want me to move too?'

I was not mapping out my own destiny anymore so never knew

what was round the corner, but God did! As I let God direct my path, things started to fit into place. The next couple that viewed my house fell in love with it, but their house was not within the boundaries of where I wanted to move too. 'Where did you say you live? Chipping where?'

I asked uneasily. It was a small town near the Cotswolds, too far away for my liking. The couple loved my place and almost begged me to look at theirs before I made any decision, so I did. Even before I saw the place, I knew in my heart of hearts God wanted me to move there. I adored the location with its fresh country air, green open spaces and cosy tea-rooms. I could truly go 'over the hills and far away' here! The swap was straight forward with no complications. Although it was only ten miles from the city, it seemed like I was going to the far side of the world. I am not an adventurous person, so it was quite a challenge for me, but Jesus supported me every step of the way. I was learning that trusting in him meant that there would never be a dull moment!

The house itself was a small two-up two-down terraced house; both house and garden needed a little work done on them, nothing major, only cosmetic (or so I thought!). It is funny what you find when folk have moved out and taken their carpets and furniture with them. However, I was not exactly laughing when I saw the

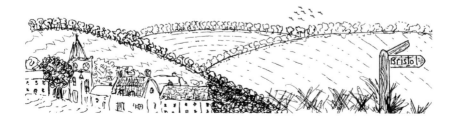

state of the rooms. The walls needed plastering, the fireplace was broken, and the doors did not fit properly. And what about the garden? The previous tenant had kept a motorbike out in the back garden; everywhere, as far as the eye could see, was dried up black oil: on the grass, the patio, the shed, even up the walls of the house. No pretty flowers or trees here. My thoughts went to my beautiful garden with a panoramic view and I had given it up for this. 'Oh, Lord, what have I done?' I cried. I recollected from previous moans and groans that self pity got you nowhere, and God gently reminded me how I had transformed gardens one and two, so now I could do the same with garden number three.

However, this time I did not have the energy or enthusiasm for it. A few months prior to my move I had been diagnosed with osteoarthritis. 'No more heavy gardening for you,' my doctor remarked. Friends thought I was crazy to move house, but I knew it was God's plan to go regardless of my circumstances. Remember, we do not allow those mountains in our lives to rule us, *we rule them*! We do not deny they exist, but we *do* deny their right to stay in our lives. I knew it was God's will for me to be in good health. Arthritis is a disease and Jesus nailed *all* diseases on that cross. As far as I was concerned, the discomfort and pain in my body was only temporary, it was not going to stay. Jesus is our healer! I could not see the arthritis gone with my human eyes, but I could through my eyes of faith. 1 Peter 2:24 says of Jesus, 'by whose stripes we were healed.' 'Stripes' referred to the beatings that Jesus was given before being nailed to the cross. 'Were' is past tense, which means Jesus has already dealt with our pain and sickness. Healing belongs to us. This is where our faith comes in, this is the evidence not yet seen. We have to *own* our healing *before* we see it. 'He took our suffering and carried our diseases,' (Matthew 8:17). Close your eyes for a moment and try to imagine that gruesome scene where the Roman soldiers beat Jesus so severely he could hardly walk. Those blood red stripes on Jesus' body were for you and me. There were

Our third garden before the makeover (left) . . . and after it is transformed (right).

My front room needed a makeover (left). The front room after the makeover (right), which was made possible due to the kindness of friends at my new church.

times when I was in so much pain, so I would remind myself what Jesus went through to give me my healing. The same as he took my guilt and shame and much more. Jesus became a living sacrifice for you and me because he loves us.

Even though healing belongs to us, we should be sensible and look after ourselves. It is important to eat properly, exercise regularly, and get a good night's sleep! All those things I did not do years ago. Look at my unhealthy lifestyle: fussy eater when a child; bulimia when a young adult; a chocoholic in my twenties and thirties. It is no wonder I suffered with diverticulitis (a disorder of the intestines) and lost some of my teeth! It was only after God healed me of M.E. during my forties that I started looking after my health. God helped me get both my health and strength back, and gave me the desire to eat nutritious foods. The difference now is that I am in control of what I eat, and not the other way round! I had a 'sweet tooth' for

The most important thing to remember is that God loves you far more than you love yourself. God does not look at our outward appearance, he looks at our hearts. He cares about our whole being: spirit, soul and body. And if we allow him to, he will change us into something pretty amazing.

years, and could not resist the chocolate, puddings, and cakes, but now that desire has gone. I used to eat a whole box of chocolates in one go, a full bag of bonbons, and fresh cream cakes (this was not related to the bulimia, as I did not make myself sick after eating such a feast). The term used is 'comfort eating,' usually associated with anxiety. People around me had no idea what was going on, they would say 'go on, have another slice of chocolate cake, you don't need to lose weight!' Why do people assume that if a person is slim, they can eat fatty foods?

Remember: it is not about the size you are, it is about *who you are* underneath that size. If you are a size twenty and have no health issues, then just enjoy being you! If you are a size eight and have no health problems, just be yourself! If you want to lose or put on weight, and it is for the right reasons, then do so. It should always be about how comfortable you feel. There are some great outfits in our shops these days, available in all sizes and reasonably priced, so go for it!

We need to encourage ourselves by believing what God says about us. Look up verses in the Bible that describe how God sees you, and what he says about you. Write them down, keep them in your diary or journal; speak the verses aloud to yourself. Do what I do and stick them on your mirror!

'I am his treasured possession.' (Exodus 19:5).

'I am the apple of his eye.' (Zechariah 2:8).

'I am precious in his sight.' (Isaiah 43:4).

'I will not leave you as orphans; I will come to you.' (John 14:18).

'As my father loves me, I love you, stay in my love.' (John 15:9).

'Your heart will be glad, and your joy no one will take from you.' (John 16:22).

When I first discovered God's incredible love for me, it blew me away! When I realised my relationship with him was not dependant on what I did, but on what Jesus did for me on the cross, it changed my life. God was saying to me, 'I love you, my daughter, even on your bad hair days.' God was not waiting for my grumpiness to go *before* his goodness would shine through me. He wanted me to come to him, grumps and all! God is the one who is working out his completed works in all of us, as we believe in him. The grumps and bad hair days will fade away as we spend time focusing on how good God is, and what his thoughts about us are. We will wake up one morning and say, 'Hey! Life is not so bad after all!' The Bible says we are God's work of art, a priceless treasure, a unique being.

Start believing what the Word (the Bible) says about you, not what the world says about you.

Chapter Fifteen
Good News

Within a short space of time, the house and garden became presentable and cosy. God sent some new friends into my life who helped me with the work, one was a plasterer, one was a plumber, and another was a painter! Once I was settled, I decided to check out the local churches. A friend wanted me to go to her church that was a few miles away in the neighbouring town. I would have preferred something local, but I went for a visit to see what it was like, and I liked what I saw! After the first few visits, you could not keep me away! It took me a while to relax and get to know people, but their genuine love and warmth won me over (no judging or pointing fingers in this place). The pastor was teaching from the Bible under the authority of the Holy Spirit. God is definitely here, I thought! Nine plus years later and I am still at this church. God knew what he was doing when he moved me out of the city!

Reuben took a little while to settle into this church. New places and faces worried him; he was only comfortable in familiar surroundings. However, one lady in particular was very kind and patient with him and offered to look after him in Sunday school. No one at this new church had witnessed my son's outbursts of frustration (and I hoped they never would!). All went well until the children started practising for the nativity play. Out came the costumes for them to try on; everyone got excited except my son. There was *no way* he was going to dress up, so they let him do the costume rehearsal without a costume! He enjoyed the rehearsals, so I was confident he would be fine doing the actual production in front of an audience. I was *so* confident that I invited some friends to come along.

The big day arrived and the stage was set; all the children went in one by one when it was their turn. Now it was Reuben's turn to go out on stage, but he hesitated.

'Come on, Reuben, you can do this,' I said.

Now it is one thing to encourage Reuben, and this is good; but it is another to push him into doing something when he has made up his mind *not* to. His outbursts were not often, but the volume of the outbursts made up for the infrequency! The children vacated the dressing room with amazing speed, while I sat and waited for my son to finish his rage. I had learnt that once Reuben 'kicked off' it was best to wait at a distance until he has finished. Before his operations, Reuben was a gentle-natured boy who showed no signs of frustration; I was still convinced it was the result of the pain and his inability to do what he used to do.

When the angry outbursts first appeared I was in fear of them, it upset me to see my boy in such a state. But when I received the peace that Jesus longed for me to have, I, in turn, was able to comfort and reassure Reuben during the quiet times. There were funny times too, once we went to the beach for the day and it was packed with holidaymakers, there was no space anywhere. I don't know if it was the heat or the crowded beach that started Reuben off, but his screams cleared a space for us in minutes!

When his outburst was over and he had calmed down, Reuben was as sweet as sugar and would want one of his 'huggles' (a hug and a cuddle!). Remember the mountain and the molehill? Both Reuben's physical and emotional conditions constituted a mountain that needed to go. Reuben was not experiencing the quality of life that Jesus had promised us. He was taking morphine-based medication, due to extreme pain in his knees. Reuben's reluctance to go up stairs and steps became a real problem. Though coming down them was a different matter, as he 'bottom-shuffled' down each step. This he loved doing!

Reuben had gained extra weight which caused his legs to become

unsteady, and there were times when he could hardly walk. He also suffered with rhinitis, a condition that affects the nasal passages, and there was talk of an operation to unblock them. 'Operation? No way!' I thought. Back to the Lord in prayer I went. Jesus said, 'Truly I tell you, if you have faith and do not doubt . . . you can say to this mountain, "Go, throw yourself into the sea," and it will be done.' (Matthew 21:21). I had stepped up from hope to faith, to a place where possibilities are born and doubts can be discarded. It was both a challenging and exciting place to be. When wrong, negative thoughts entered my head, I started focusing on the opposite of that thought. Faith gives us the assurance that all is well regardless of what we can see, it makes us feel stronger and healthier on the inside. Some of you may already be optimistic about everything that comes your way, and so think you do not need faith in God to steer you through life. Your accountability and dependence is in yourself, but have you ever thought where this will lead you? *Are you so self-assured and confident that you know what the future holds for you and your family?*

Reuben bottom-shuffling down the stairs.

Reuben's healing came in a very practical way. My friend remarked that her daughter had changed from dairy products to soya and had not suffered a cold since. I mentioned this next time I saw the ear, nose and throat specialist and he said, 'Give it a try.' So I replaced dairy for soya in Reuben's diet, and within six months a remarkable change took place. He stopped having chesty colds and even lost weight! I believe God prompted that friend to speak to me. This is often how it works; it is not always dynamics from the sky, but sometimes it can be. We should welcome both the ordinary and the extraordinary! Expectancy grew in me as my faith in God's promises began coming to pass. I changed from *wanting* to believe in my son's healing, to *knowing* it belonged to him. I now know that my son is going to hear and speak with full understanding. My faith in Reuben's health and well-being is based on what Jesus has *already* done. Watch this space!

You can have healing for you and your family too, if only you would believe.

Life brings all sorts of stuff our way, some good, some bad and some ugly. As I have said before, how we deal with this stuff, and how we react to it, will affect our journey. Life was about to change for Reuben dramatically. The transition stage from school to the community became a challenging time for him. The day centres were few and far between, and colleges had limited places and subjects; so Reuben began 'life after school' at home with me. Within a few months, the community care team found a placement one day a week at a day centre. 'Better than nothing,' I thought; but even this one day proved too much for Reuben! He disliked the place so much that he would be reluctant to get off the mini bus that took him there. The bus driver would be waiting to drive away, not knowing what to do. The day centre would ring up asking me to collect him. This happened on several occasions. That car park became a familiar place to me! When I arrived, Reuben was very distressed, so I sang to him, 'I can see you are not happy so let's call it a day, come home with me and we can pray.' Reuben loved it when I sang to him, so responded to my offer gladly! Reuben was not used to his new surroundings, they upset him and he kept asking to go back to school. He had been happy at school, now everything had changed and we had to start all over again. Weeks turned into months as I continued to trust God that something would turn up. During the next few years, Reuben tried and rejected more day centres and support agencies than I got through hot dinners! Seriously, he never could settle; he was still missing the security and comfort of school life. One day I asked God, 'Lord, please let there be somewhere that Reuben will be happy,' and he answered me. This time it was a small, private daycare facility, not a large day centre, and was run by a very friendly couple way out in the country on a farm! It was a working farm with sheep, tractors and even a lake with fish!

This couple were extremely understanding and welcomed Reuben with open arms from day one. They let me stay with him until he settled in. One day a week progressed to two, three and sometimes four days a week over the following years. Reuben took to the farm like a duck to water; and at the time of writing, he is still there! He sees them as his aunty and uncle, and helps pack his bags to go and stay with them for an occasional night's respite. I say a big 'thank you' to a wonderful, caring couple who have always supported and loved my son as if he were their own. I so appreciate all that you have done for us, may the Lord richly bless you and your family. Whilst attending the farm, Reuben became more relaxed, so I enrolled him into some short college courses; his favourite was dance, drama, and music. He can be quite shy, but when you put a microphone in his hand, Reuben comes alive! At church, school and college his talents have been on display for all to see.

At last we found a day placement that Reuben was happy with—on a farm!

Reuben singing in church.

Reuben proudly receives his certificate for completing a six-week cookery course.

Chapter Sixteen
Amazing Grace

One Sunday morning I woke early; the arthritic pain in my back having caused me to have a disturbed night. For a year, I had been sleeping flat on my back with only one or even no pillow. I longed for the day when I would sleep curled up on my side with two fluffy pillows! I lived in expectation of this happening. That morning I was lead to read James 5:14–15:

> Is anyone among you sick? Let him call for the elders of the church, and let them pray over him, anointing him with oil in the name of the Lord. And the prayer of faith will save the one who is sick, and the Lord will raise him up. . . .

'Anointing with oil' is not referring to a medicinal remedy, but a symbol of the Holy Spirit. When it is applied in prayer using Jesus' name, we will see the power and presence of God at work. I knew those verses from the Bible, but they had made no impression on me until that day. God spoke to me through those verses and he wanted me to do what they said! I was not keen to do this so answered him, 'Lord, I know it is your will for me to be healed of my pain, but does it have to be in front of everybody in church?' I still lacked confidence with large crowds. I wanted healing in my own home.

This is what I sensed God gave me in his reply, 'Your healing is about my son being glorified in you. There are times for healing to take place when you are alone, and there are times for healing to take place in front of others. This is what I want for you. It is about my son being glorified in you.'

Wow! It all became so clear. In the Bible Jesus went around doing good and healing everybody. He told some folk not to broadcast their healing, but others he told to go out and share what had happened to them. I realised I wanted healing on my own terms. When I reacted in a *self*-centred manner, I had taken my eyes off the healer, the very one who should be the centre of my life—Jesus. When we allow our *soul* (mind, will and emotions) to be in charge, then the *self* will have a paddy! That morning I had a paddy and looked back to how I used to be; I used to be shy and hated being in large gatherings, it all scared me. But then I remembered what Jesus had done to remove my shyness and fears; I saw a new person who was *not* shy or scared. I had a new identity in him! There is a lovely song that starts off like this, 'Jesus, be the centre of my life.' Not in a corner, not in a box, not in some distant, far off place; but slap, bang in the centre of our lives! That morning I learnt so much. I was beginning to see how big and awesome Jesus really was; I was growing up. We all begin this life as babies, then we become children, and then adults; this is mirrored in our spiritual lives. Babies need milk, but adults require solid food.

Reuben and I went to church and I had great expectations in my heart. Reuben loved the church as he sensed the relaxed atmosphere, and enjoyed the praise and worship music. Towards the end of the service, *self* reared up in me producing fear. 'No way!' I thought, I am a new creation and old things have passed away. The fear soon shut up! Then a thought came into my head, 'They don't use oil for healing here.' I should have remembered the powerful time I had spent with my Lord that very morning, but I did not. I waited for the pastor to call people out for prayer for healing, but he did not. Maybe he will mention the oil, I thought; but he did not utter a word. Oh dear! The service had ended and I could see the pastor making his way down the aisle. 'Help, Lord, what shall I do?' I thought. What happened next is hard for the human mind to comprehend; it was as if a strong wind pushed me out from where I stood to where the pastor was! It reminded me of an incident from years before, when my sister was teaching me to ride a bike. She had been guiding me all afternoon, holding onto the rear seat; then with one mighty push she let go and I went speeding down the field! There I was, standing eyeball to eyeball with my pastor, blurting out, 'Do you use oil when you pray for healing?' I cannot remember his reply, but he took me to the platform where the oil was and prayed for me. The answer to your question, 'Did I get healed?' is 'Yes, I did!' That night I curled up with two fluffy pillows and slept like a baby.

Lord, I am *so* appreciative of what you have done for me. When I get to heaven I want to give you a big hug, though I expect the queues for hugs will be tremendous, so I will have to wait my turn!

If you are sick and want to be healed, please understand that Jesus is your healer and wants you to be well. Sometimes it is instant and sometimes it is a recovery process. Do not give up, it will come to pass.

Queue
for hugs
here.

We can all experience a better quality of life with Jesus. In John 10:10, Jesus says: 'I came that they may have life and have it abundantly.' *Abundant: Overflowing, generous, plentiful, more than enough!* It has taken me well over forty years to discover this quality of life. Please do not let it take you even half as long. I am now able to face the challenges and surprises life brings me because I know who I am. My identity is in Jesus, I belong to him and he values me. My very existence is precious and important to him. If I fall down, I will get up again; if today has been difficult, tomorrow will be better.

Chapter Seventeen
Baptism

A few years before we moved to the country, Reuben came to me saying, 'Baptise—water, baptise—water.' He had seen his brothers get baptised, also other people in the church doing the same. I thought Reuben was not ready for this, but I was *so* wrong! That same day Reuben repeatedly sang a song he had learnt, 'Into my heart, come into my heart, Lord Jesus. Come in today, come in to stay, come into my heart, Lord Jesus.' I then realised it was Reuben's way of giving his life to Jesus; he sang his way into Jesus' heart.

After all the arrangements had been made, the big day finally arrived. I had invited many friends to attend as it was to be an exciting occasion. That day was truly a day to remember; Reuben stepped in front of the microphone on stage and sang his song again. My main concern was that Reuben might take off and start swimming in the baptismal pool (he loves swimming) but he did not. He stood in that pool letting them pray over him, and allowed them to dip him under the water and up again! Reuben knew what he was doing that day and it was all captured on video!

Baptism in water is a practical outward sign saying, 'I am going to follow Jesus from now on.' It represents saying goodbye to our old way of life (going under the water) and saying hello to our new one (coming back up) It is not a sprinkling of water on the forehead, but total submersion for a few seconds. Jesus said, 'Whoever believes and is baptised will be saved,' (Mark 16:16). A baby has no understanding of

Reuben singing 'Come into My Heart, Lord Jesus' at his baptism service.

Jesus, therefore it would be wise to wait until it is old enough to make the decision to be baptised itself. However, many people like to dedicate their babies to God in a church service. This is showing God they want their children to grow up in the knowledge of him. However, this is not an assurance that the child will believe in him when they get to an age when they can reason; what they choose to believe will be up to them. We, as parents, can only pray that our offspring will discover the truth.

'We baptise you in the name of the Father, the Son and the Holy Spirit'

'Goodbye old life. Hello new one!'

Jesus also said, '. . . whoever loses his life for my sake will find it.' (Matthew 10:39). This means there is a whole new way of life out there waiting for us if we would *only believe*. It is God's will for everybody to know him in a personal way, and to receive his loving kindness. God wants us to call him 'Father'. When we cross over from unbelieving to believing this Father adopts us as his own, we become his sons and daughters! We can only come to the Father through Jesus. Jesus made this possible through his death, burial and resurrection. Jesus destroyed the works of the evil one so everybody could have the opportunity to find the truth. We are all aware of the existence of evil in this world, but do not want to believe there is a force behind it. The only thing we can agree on, is that we want evil to leave for good.

Let me share a few facts about the evil one. He has many names and disguises and too much publicity. The Bible refers to him as the false god of this world and the devil, (note small *g* and *d*.) The world has been conditioned not to believe in a devil; if only they realised he put that idea around in the first place! Fear is his *only* weapon, as he has no other power whatsoever; he uses fear tactics to spread lies around the world and discord amongst people. The evil one began his life on earth sowing seeds of shame, guilt and fear into the first humans. The evil one messed up their lives because he was jealous of their relationship with God. They listened to his lies and ate from that out-of-bounds tree. We tell our children 'do not put your fingers in the sockets' or 'stay on the path,' and they go and do the opposite. I was the same throughout much of my life, listening to nonsense instead of common sense. The first humans did the same thing; one minute they were relaxing and enjoying freedom with the creator of this universe, then next minute they sensed shame and fear so hid from him, all because they listened to the lies of the evil one. The beautiful relationship with God and humans was broken that day and the connection was lost. Even though that connection was broken, God did not give up on them. In 1 John 3:8, 'The one who practices sin is of the devil, because the devil has been sinning from the beginning. For this purpose the Son of God was revealed: to destroy the works of the devil.' God brought his son, Jesus, to restore that broken relationship between man and God. He does not want anyone to live in fear because his very nature is opposite to this. He is a God of love and peace and longs for our hand of friendship instead of hostility. In him, there is a place of safety, we come empty handed with souls full of heartache. He fills our hands with good things and restores our souls! If we could all wake up to the fact that there *is* a God that has our best interests at heart, then his love would flourish amongst us like seedlings on a warm spring morning!

Can you call God your father? He is waiting to call you his son or daughter.

Enjoying the sunshine in-between meetings at a Christian event in the Midlands with two very precious friends.

My lovely sisters who both know Jesus.

Chapter Eighteen
All Things Are Possible

One day my thoughts turned to going back to work. Reuben was settling in well at the farm, so I had more time on my hands. I thought shop work would be best, so off I went round the shops asking if they needed anybody. They looked at me as if I was an alien from another planet; a CV was required with references, just to do a few hours a week! They also wanted someone to work 'flexi' hours, which involved weekends. My CV was ancient, and weekends were out of the question, so I opted for a voluntary job in the local charity shop (I think they took pity on me when they realised I had been traipsing round all day for work!). The first day I worked there, I heard the shop was closing down within two months! It was not a concern to me, but some of the staff had been there for years and were very upset. I enjoyed my time spent at the shop and made some new friends.

At home, I was talking with the Lord, asking him what to do; should I go to another charity shop? The answer came through an article in the local newspaper: 'Making a Difference'. It was a ten-week course for people who had been out of the workplace for a long time (me!). The venue was at the local community centre. By the autumn I found myself sitting around an oversized table with nine other people, wondering what I was doing there. My mind tried to remind me of the 'old days' when my crippling shyness

I want to go home!

prevented me from looking folk in the eye. When I would go a shade of pink, have the shakes and sweat profusely!

It was only for a moment that those thoughts came back to me, and I was not going to listen to them. I reminded myself of who I was, and where I was heading! 'My life is in Jesus now,' I told myself, 'I will not entertain wrong thoughts.' God was with me and would guard my mind; those old nerves soon left for good! I thoroughly enjoyed the course and met some lovely people with whom I have still kept in touch. After the first course, I gained confidence to pursue further studies, so I brushed up on both English and maths. Maths was a non-starter, but English was good. It was great to get my brain cells motivated again and I was looking forward to finding employment. However, this never happened, as life put another obstacle across my path; *but this time I was prepared!*

It all began when I noticed Reuben was struggling to keep his food down. Some foods he found difficult to digest, so I started chopping and mashing the food into bite size portions. I prayed from day one, asking God to show me what was causing it; also speaking God's promises over Reuben for a long, healthy life. Reuben's doctor thought it might be an allergy of some kind; so I carefully monitored what Reuben ate, noting the foods his stomach was rejecting. In the meantime, the doctor arranged for Reuben to see a specialist. Reuben normally loved his food, so he was not a happy chappy. He became quite weak and his legs were giving way, making him reluctant to attempt the stairs. To begin with I used the commode for him, keeping it in the downstairs hall, but this proved unsatisfactory; so I decided to keep Reuben in his bedroom, making him as comfortable as possible.

When our minds scream 'Impossible!' out of our spirits we hear a different cry, 'Possible with God.' Obstacles will be removed and breakthroughs will come, because we are *with God*. 'Jesus . . . said, "With man this is impossible, but not with God. For all things are possible with God." (Mark 10:27). This assurance kept me going, so I kept Reuben going! That bedroom became a fun place to be as I sang, danced and did activities with him. We should never lose sight of that rainbow and never allow our present circumstances to control our future. No matter how bleak our situation appears, there is always hope for change. As I have mentioned before, clinging onto the anchor of hope will bring us to that place of safety. *Never let go and never give up.*

Nursing Reuben back to full health took all my time and energy, but I was not the weak, negative mum I used to be. I rolled my sleeves up and just got on with it, knowing it was temporary and it would be over very soon. Anyway, going up and down those stairs every day kept me fit! I was sitting in my kitchen one morning with a friend, enjoying a cup of tea and a chat when she suggested I apply for a bungalow. The thought had crossed my mind some years before, but I had done nothing about it. I did not want to home swap again, so contacted my housing association. Within a month my name was put on a waiting list to move. While hoping for the bungalow to materialise, I remained firmly convinced that Reuben would make a full recovery wherever we lived. If we did move into a bungalow there would be no restrictions for Reuben. God has our best interests at heart and will guide and support us through this life if we let him. After seeing the specialist, it was decided that Reuben would have to spend a day in hospital for tests. He was to have to have a laprascotomy, which involved a camera being inserted down his throat and fed into his stomach. Reuben would have to be sedated, and remembering from past experiences, I knew this would *not* be easy! When I found a quiet moment on my own, I prayed, 'Jesus, this healing and peace you have provided for us, belongs to Reuben too. I thank you that Reuben will not suffer pain or discomfort, and will get better very soon.'

The day arrived for Reuben's appointment; he responded well to the sedation with no outbursts, and slept like a baby! We even came home the same day. What a friend we have in Jesus!

The results revealed a stomach ulcer, poor thing, no wonder Reuben had found it a struggle to keep his food down. The word 'operation' was mentioned, 'Oh no, not again!' I cried. That ulcer had no rights to be in my son's stomach, it had to go, but an operation? The next few days I spent time with God asking for his wisdom in the matter. I went back to see the specialist intending to tell him that I could not put Reuben through the trauma of any more operations, but before I had a chance to speak, he gave me good news! He told me that some ulcers are eradicated by medication, but not all, so if I was willing, we could give it a try. Over the next few months both prayers and medication sent messages to the ulcer, giving it its marching orders. Reuben was amazing, he had come to understand he could not have certain foods, suffered no side effects from the medicine, and became his happy self. The plan was to gradually introduce certain foods into his diet and increase the amounts. Reuben made a full recovery, and was eating his favourite pasta meals within months! I thank God for medicines, treatment and the medical profession. Medical care can relieve suffering and prolong a person's life. Surgeons, doctors and nurses need all the prayers we can send; they do amazing work under tremendous pressure these days. Sometimes operations and treatment are necessary for our recovery and healing, other times they are not. It is very important that we do the right thing. I believe God empowers surgeons to perform delicate operations, and influences scientists to develop certain medicines to save lives. With good health care people are living longer, giving them the opportunity to hear the good news that only Jesus brings. We should never despise or reject medical treatment. Look at the third world countries; these places need basic sanitation, food, fresh drinking water, and medical supplies just to survive and function properly. All the stuff we in the Western countries take for granted or even moan about. Charities and organisations from around the world do tireless, commendable work to alleviate suffering. Some are Christian-based and do the same work as the other charities, but can also share the good news of Jesus. Every man, woman and child, regardless of age, disability, nationality, culture, or status has the right to hear the truth. Even on our death beds it is not too late to hear the truth and respond to it.

This was taken at a time when Reuben couldn't walk, so I made his bedroom a fun place to be.

Chapter Nineteen
From Rags to Riches

Plans to move to a bungalow meant downsizing; my house was bulging at the seams with stuff, so it could do with going on a diet! Somebody once said to me, 'Georgina, because you cannot fill that emptiness in your heart, you have to fill your home.' I was not sure what they meant, but now I did. I had been an avid collector of all things great and small for a number of years, including teddy bears, vintage tins and teapots. The desire to collect things had now lost its appeal, so I was able to let them all go (to good homes!). However, there were still black bin sacks full of fabrics, lace, ribbons, and bits and bobs from my rag trade days.

One morning, I was sorting out stuff in my bedroom, separating and making signs for each pile: recycling, charity shop and rubbish. I was still reluctant to part with the fabric bags as I was convinced they would come in useful one day. That day was going to be sooner than I thought! 'Any ideas what I can do with them, Lord?' He certainly had! It says in the Bible that God directs and guides us where we should go, and this is exactly what he did for me. He directed me to a craft fair held in the town hall. There was so much to see, beautifully designed crafts from knitted cupcakes to hand painted watering cans, it was amazing! The idea to make hand-made items from my ragbags was born that day. I started making fabric cards and giving them to friends and family. Then I went on to make rag dolls, aprons, bags and much more. Old-fashioned wooden clothes pegs were great to convert into little angels for the Christmas tree. Almost everything I used was from remnants or recycled stuff. My first stall was in my house at Christmas, in aid of a charity we supported at church. It was an amazing success.

With the Lord's help, I gained confidence and was able to sell my crafts at local fairs and markets. The Lord encouraged and inspired me throughout the whole time. One day he spoke to me, telling me to give every penny I earned from the sale of my crafts to charity, so I did. From that day to this, I have not experienced lack in my finances. God is good, *all* the time! As I have said before, hearing from God is not usually an audible voice one hears with one's natural ears (though I am not denying this can happen) but that still, small voice from within (our conscience). When we learn to believe and trust in God, our conscience will listen to him instead of to rubbish! Friends joined me in my fundraising efforts for various charities. In time, I partnered with some friends who were making and selling crafts themselves and we jointly raised money for an orphanage and school in Africa. Every sale was a success.

Are you a hoarder or collector of stuff? Do you have it under control or does it control you? Can you let it go?

My dolly-peg angels.

With a friend at a Victorian fair in Chipping Sodbury (I look like Mrs Tiggywinkle!).

The day before Christmas Eve I was reminiscing about when my four sons were little, and the days leading up to Christmas Day were full of anticipation and excitement. Their faces glowed with joy, shouting 'Go on, Mum, tell us another story!' I often shared Christmas stories with them, some from my own childhood and some I made up. Christmas in the 1950s was very different to what it is now! In our home when I was small, money was scarce, but love was plentiful. At Christmas our house was so warm and cosy with an open fire, and paper chains and lanterns hanging from the ceiling. Mother made us presents and new frocks to wear on Christmas day. One year, she made me a doll's house out of cardboard boxes, complete with furniture and curtains, it was beautiful. Sometimes she had to work over the Christmas period, which I found difficult. My dad and mum gave up running the hotel when I was a small child due to dad's poor health, so mum worked in another hotel as a waitress. She worked long and late hours and Christmas was an especially busy time for her. I would stand watching and waiting at the window for hours, longing to see her coming home from her shifts. Though weary and worn out, mum still managed a smile and a hug for us girls when she walked through the front door. Often she came back with some tasty titbits. We girls would gather excitedly around the kitchen table to feast on the delights set before us! Small iced fondant cakes wrapped in pretty paper doilies were my favourites. Despite mum having to work so many hours, she still made time to give us an amazing Christmas. I wanted to do the same for my sons when they were young, but I was not as talented. Every year I got the boys involved in making Christmas decorations; out came the craft box containing cardboard toilet rolls, cotton wool and buttons to make the Nativity figures. When they were young, the boys loved cutting, gluing and colouring crafts for Christmas, but as they grew older they recoiled from such activities. The year my sons cried out in unison, 'Not the dreaded toilet rolls, anything but that!' I realised it was the end of an era!

'Oh no!'

Reuben still adores Christmas time, so I turn his room into a shimmering grotto complete with twinkling lights and snow figures. He loves *The Snowman* film, and watches it over and over again, so once Christmas ends I have to hide it! However, Christmas should never end in our hearts as we can embrace its real meaning by celebrating the birth of Jesus. Let the nativity scene take pride of place in your homes (it does not have to be handmade!) and sit and reflect why that baby came into the world. Absorb the words of the carols sung in churches, school halls and on television. Take *him* out of Christmas and what are we left with? *Crstas.*

Christmas can be a very difficult time of year for many people. Emotions get churned up as we remember departed loved ones. If one does not have family or friends around it can make one feel isolated. Even in some churches (not all) the emphasis seems to be on 'happy families' instead of Jesus' birthday. I was one of those lonely people once. I suffered with an inferiority complex that made me view Christmas through a distorted lens.

Every year, in church, folk would come with piles of cards in their hands giving them out to certain individuals. Was I invisible or didn't they know me well enough? Whatever it was, I hardly ever received any cards. Back then it affected me terribly, making me feel unwanted. I had not yet learned how important and valuable

I was to God. Some churches need to share this truth, and become more sensitive and understanding to the vulnerable and displaced who walk through their doors.

It is *only* through God's loving care for me that I am free now. In my church, these days, I send *one card* to the whole congregation! After all, we are supposed to be a part of one big family worldwide, God's family, so let us start acting like one.

I had just finished wrapping up Reuben's Christmas presents, when the news came. A bungalow was available to view, and I was next on the list! I phoned the office and they said I could look at it that very day. A housing officer took me in her car to look at it; she said I only had until Christmas Eve to reject or accept the property. 'But that is tomorrow!' I told her, 'That does not give me enough time to think about it.' She told me it was not company policy to leave the place empty for too long, and there were others on the list that would want it if I did not. I could see her point, but there was so little time to decide. As we drove up to the entrance, I silently said to God, 'Lord, I need your wisdom here.' He already knew the bungalow was mine, and once I went inside and looked around, so did I! It was very clean and freshly painted (no plastering to do here!) We went out through the back door to a rather small garden, overgrown with brambles. This time I did not raise an eyebrow in despair, but said quietly, 'It is okay, Lord, I am fine with this.' The bonus was that my church was only round the corner, so I went to the housing office to accept their offer, and they told me I had two weeks to vacate my house. Those two weeks were chaotic and exciting; I was undressing the Christmas tree on Boxing Day!

My journey was looking good; at last I could roll down the window and breathe in fresh air. After moving to the bungalow I continued designing and sewing at my kitchen table (no spare room.) God was blessing the work of my hands and I was so grateful to him. One day I asked God to bless Reuben's ability to learn new skills. Reuben's abilities were very limited, as he had always been reluctant to do things outside his comfort zone (I think we can all relate to this!). Reuben could speak, but did not volunteer this with enthusiasm, sometimes he would go a whole week with no verbal communication. The only way I could get him to respond was through singing, every task we did was in song. For instance, when it was time for Reuben to clean his teeth, I would sing: 'Let us clean our teeth together, and we will feel much better!' I woke one morning with the idea that if Reuben could read, then speech would follow! This sounds back to front, but this has actually become a reality in Reuben's life, and all credit goes to a wonderful God who gave me the idea. I made a set of teaching aids to encourage Reuben's communication skills, spending hours cutting and colouring every letter, word and sentence in card with Velcro backing. As anyone who knows anything about Velcro knows, it can get 'hairy', so I had them completely redone in laminate with

a magnetic backing. The laminate idea was a good one, but costly. At the time, I was receiving money for Reuben through the direct payment scheme, which paid for his day care. I always had some surplus left at the end of each month, and the policy was to give it back. I approached the social services to see if I could use the surplus for teaching aids for Reuben. After a visit from a speech and language therapist to see the work I was doing with him, they agreed! Within two years there were large magnetic whiteboards adorning the walls of our home, complete with sets of colour-coded words and letters. Reuben can now identify, pronounce and spell certain words. It has opened up a new world for him and he is so proud of his achievements. Friends remark, 'Oh, I did not know Reuben could speak,' and 'Was that Reuben; he sounded so clear?' Yes, it certainly was!

Reuben has started his own journey of discovery. He is friendly and sociable, and learning to cope well with new places and faces. Although Reuben still uses the wheelchair outdoors when he gets tired, his walking has greatly improved. A few years ago Reuben had x-rays taken on his knees to see if there was any arthritis present (I was praying, and believed that there would *not* be) the report came back with no trace whatsoever! This was all due to a good God who wanted the best for us. We are worth something to him. No other prophet or religious leader throughout the centuries has promised or delivered such declarations as Jesus has. *Declaration: statement, testimony.* None of them laid down their lives for the sake of their followers in order for them to be forgiven, free, healed and have everlasting life. Go and study the history books for yourselves.

At the end of eight years, my craft making days came to a close, as I sensed God was about to lead me in a new direction. I laid down my needles, scissors and threads for the last time. I loved doing those craft fairs, especially the vintage ones! But it was time for a change. With simple, childlike trust I would follow God, and am still doing so as I write. In our own strength, we can do nothing. Jesus said, 'I am the vine. You are the branches. He who remains in me, and I in him, bears much fruit, for apart from me you can do nothing.' (John 15:5).

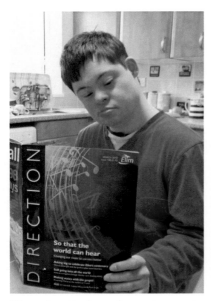

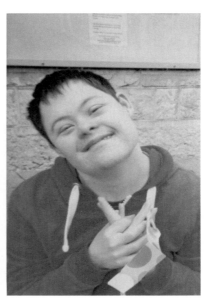

These days Reuben takes an interest in reading.

When Reuben smiles, he lights up our lives.

Chapter Twenty
In Him We Live

When life appears good and we are running on a full tank, sometimes we forget to chill out and breathe! 'I think I have taken on too much,' and 'I find it hard to say no' were phrases which rang true for me in early 2013. I was here, there and everywhere! People, places and things had been taking up all my time and energy.

It is good to pursue work and leisure activities, but *not* to the extent that one feels exhausted at the end of each day. I believe God will show us what to take on and what to let go of if we let him. I sensed God was prompting me to slow down and take stock of my situation. One by one, I was able to let go of things that had been 'taking over.' Not heavy burdens as in my past, but stuff that had appeared good at the time. Even Good Samaritan deeds can take their toll on us. I was busy helping folk, but I should have realised that I cannot take on the world. I had been running all over the place doing stuff, after I had said I would never do that again. God was waiting for me to talk to him about my busy life. I felt safe and secure knowing he was by my side at all times; but there is always more to discover about him, as I was about to find out.

One afternoon I said, 'Please, Lord, show me who to help in the future.' As I sat there, I sensed a beautiful peace and was overwhelmed with our Father's love towards me. It may be hard to understand, but he longs to be a father to us. I sensed he wanted me to pursue him at a deeper level *before* I embarked on saving the world! Beautiful verses from the Bible stirred my heart: 'Be still, and know that I am God,' (Psalm 46:10). 'My Presence will go with you, and I will give you rest.' (Exodus 33:14).

The senior citizens among us will remember the song 'Getting to Know You' with its lyrics 'Getting to know you; Getting to know all about you.' This is what I had started to do; I knew God, but did not know all about him, and there was a difference. He wanted me to rest in his presence and love. Not love of the human kind, but a love above and beyond our imagination. God's love towards us is a mystery we cannot understand. Until we believe in him, we cannot experience this love. Remember the parcel on the doorstep? We have to believe to receive! Even some Christians have yet to embrace the atmosphere of pure love which is beyond that of man. We need to take a rain check on our busy schedule; even social gatherings and activities connected to church, as lovely as they are, can prevent us from pursing God's presence. Every church has a social calendar; but how many days on that calendar are set aside for purely worshipping an awesome God who puts *us* first on *his* calendar? When Jesus walked this earth, his primary concern was to do his father's will. When we walk the earth, what is our primary concern?

From the spring of 2013, my journey took me places I had never been before. I entered into a place of worship of God that was incredibly breathtaking, in fact there are no words to describe this place. The welcome mat on the doorstep, and the sign on the door said, 'Come on in!' I walked through the door and left the boundaries of time behind, I had entered a place where worship reigned and truth ruled. My soul remained speechless while my spirit sang love songs to the Father. From that day onwards, I entered into a deeper relationship with God. When we truly worship God through our spirit, we will find this place. Some of you have discovered this place a long time ago, probably when I was working out what *hope* meant! But others among you have never experienced the human kind of love, let alone the God kind. My history of being loved, and giving out love is slightly obscure. My mother and sister's love towards me was good; but my dad appeared distant and stern, though not cruel or unkind. He was much older than my mum and so was more like a granddad to me. I grew up not really as close to him as I had hoped. After three daughters, I was the child that should have been a boy, the son he so longed for. I sensed I was a disappointment to him. 'George' was to be the boy's name, so when I came along instead he just added 'Gina'. I disliked my name for a long time, as it was always a reminder of his loss. As I became an adult, I continued to disappoint the men in my life, and after two failed marriages I felt unlovable. I loved my sons, but I failed to keep us together. I blamed myself for every damaged relationship: father/daughter, husband/wife, mother/son.

Even after I was born again I could not fully understand God's love and care for me. It was not until years later, when God breathed life back into me, that I accepted his love. It was like waking up from a bad dream and being so grateful it was not real! I was a little shaky at first, but I woke up to the fact that God is good and he likes me. When Jesus bled to death on that cross because he loves me, it dawned in my heart that I must have meant a lot to him. At last I was free of guilt and the feeling of being unworthy—hurray!

No matter how unloved you may be feeling right now, no matter how much hate you may be carrying around with you, God wants to take it from you and give you his love. He has enough love to share with everybody. That pain, that ugly deep ache inside of you, I tell you the truth, no human can make it go away. Only God can relieve your suffering. He suffered on your behalf. Cry out to him. He will come to you.

God wants us to call him 'Father' and for some of us that will be very difficult. Either we had issues with our own fathers, or we have never known them. The truth is we should not compare a human father with a spiritual one, the same as we should not compare human love with spiritual love. The difference is that one is not perfect, but the other is. We are not expected to be perfect, but we should believe and look to the one that is. God the Father will do the perfecting in us, if we let him. I hope that what I have been sharing with you has not been too much for you to take in. I am just an ordinary, average person who stumbled and struggled my way through life until I found that rainbow! If I can find it, anyone can. Go, search for yourself. People that I am acquainted with these days have no idea of my past history (they will after reading this book!). They say passing remarks such as 'Oh, it is okay for you, you have got it easy,' and 'You don't know what I am going through.' My life these days is neither easy nor hard. Read the next chapter for answers.

Chapter Twenty-One
Life is for Living

When we enter into a relationship with Jesus, he gives us an unshakable confidence to cope with whatever life throws at us. I am witness to this as I have tried it out and it works! This incredible joy and peace I now experience, are in my spirit *not* my soul, and are not influenced by my circumstances. When trouble comes my way, I will not fall apart as I used to because I can draw from my spirit what is necessary for each day. This applies to every believer in Jesus. It does not mean we go round with a fixed cheesy grin all day long (although it would do some folk good to smile!) but it means we have a coping strategy in God and not in ourselves. It is *not* a crutch, in fact we can achieve far more with him than without him. A catalogue of stuff started coming my way the moment I got serious and sat down to write this book (now why am I not surprised?).

I was having my usual six-monthly dental check up, when the dentist noticed something unusual in my gums so referred me to the dental hospital, despite having no pain or discomfort. Christmas was only a month away so an appointment was booked for the following year. I thought no more about it as I was looking forward to Christmas Day because Reuben and I were going out with friends—no cooking for me that day! Christmas Day soon arrived, and eight of us sat down to enjoy a four-course meal at our local restaurant. It all happened so quickly, one minute I was chatting with our friends, the next minute hot tomato soup was in my lap! At first I did not realise the seriousness of what had occurred, as I was more concerned for my lovely new frock; I rushed to the ladies' room to clean it as best I could. It was here that I noticed my hand was very red and had gone numb, but still I did not give it much thought. I went back to the table, and as I sat down pain went up my arm. Looking down it was evident there was something wrong with my hand and wrist. My friend helped wrap wet paper towels on them; this aroused the manager's attention, and all too soon it was obvious that medical attention was needed. Reuben, who was sitting next to me, was holding up a very red finger. He, to, had not been spared that hot red liquid. The medical centre was literally next door, so off we all went to 'be seen to.' As I got outside the restaurant, I told the waitress I was going to say some words she may not understand. She told me not to worry, and said I could swear as much as I liked. Imagine her surprise when I began speaking God's word about healing over myself! What a sight we must have looked to passers by, the waitress escorting me in my red-stained dress, supporting my arm with wet napkins. Reuben was escorted by our friend who had grabbed the water jug off the table, plunging his finger into it. I heard someone cry, 'Ooooh, look at all that blood!' Can you imagine the scene?

It was very quiet in the medical centre. The staff were very helpful, acted swiftly and were grateful for our company! The outcome for me was first degree burns, but for Reuben, bless him, just a sore finger. He coped very well throughout his ordeal, I think he enjoyed the fuss made of him. After they bandaged us up and dosed us with paracetamol, we went on our way rejoicing! I went home to change (well, would *you* have stayed the whole day smelling of tomato soup?) I soon rejoined my friends to enjoy lovely fellowship and tasty food. It was not the end of the world and did not spoil our day. The peace and joy that was resident in my spirit kept me going. Read Colossians 1:11 and Philippians 3:9.

The new year brought us 2014. I attended my appointment at the hospital. The inside of my mouth became quite an attraction as not one or two, but four different medics came to stare into it! When folk get up close and personal, I tend to go cross-eyed; so have learnt the best line of defence is to close them. Then they remark, 'Are you okay?' concerned I have drifted into a deep slumber. The verdict came back that a white mass had appeared in my mouth, so I would need a biopsy. They told me I was showing signs of gum disease, not the usual common type of gum disease, but the one that carried the possibility of cancer. My thoughts went back to all those boiled sweets I had when I was a child, those sherbet lollies on a stick, I would suck them in my mouth for hours! When I told the doctor this, she assured me it is not always about what we eat, but how thorough we are at cleaning our teeth. Flossing was unheard of when I was young, my mother used to say 'An apple a day will keep the doctor away,' and when I asked what would keep the dentist away, she would reply, 'Another apple!'

When I got home, I sat down and read the leaflet they had given me; if it was cancer the outcome did not look good. Then I read my Bible. I read God's promises to his people, promises to protect us and not to harm us. To give us a long life, removing diseases, and rescuing us from destruction. After reading these amazing promises there was *no way* I would let cancer take hold of me and destroy my life! We should all live, eat and breathe under the power of the cross, not for our own agendas and through our strengths, but for and through God's. This is what I did, I dismissed negative thoughts such as 'What if it is cancer?' from my mind, told nobody, and believed I would have a good report back from the hospital.

The biopsy itself was not a nice thing to have done. The stitches in my mouth gave me a lot of discomfort. I could not manage my usual meals or hot drinks, so lived on natural yogurt and honey for a month. Despite the sore mouth and not being able to eat properly, I carried on as normal. When the results of my biopsy came back, there was not a trace of cancer! Some of you are thinking there was no evidence of cancer there in the first place, and you are absolutely right! The problem came when I was told there *may* be a possibility of cancer; should I go home and allow that negative possibility to become a reality in my life? Should I be consumed with 'what ifs' and 'maybes' to such an extent that I become convinced I have cancer? After reading that leaflet and before reading my Bible, there was a fleeting moment when doubts clouded my rational thinking. They took me down memory lane to when my mother was sick with cancer; then reminded me when my sister had a brush with cancer. I remembered even further back to when I was a child, learning that my gran had died from cancer. My mind tried to play tricks with me saying, 'It runs in the family, you cannot do anything about it.' Oh, but I can! I will *not* give cancer or any other sickness the time of day. Jesus has paid the price for sickness and pain and I believe this. However, *if* a time came in my life that I was caught off guard and sickness invaded my body, I would *still* be free because I have heaven to look forward too! I stepped from death to life the moment I asked Jesus into my life, *not* when I started believing in healing. Salvation and healing belong together, but it took me years to understand this.

A dear friend of mine went to heaven in her early forties, far too soon to leave this earth. She was a new believer and had not yet opened all the gifts Jesus had given her, and one of those gifts was healing. However, in that short space of time, she radiated God's love to everybody she met. His name was on her lips and her heart was full of joy. She may have arrived early into heaven, but she touched more people's lives with the love of Jesus in the two years that she was a Christian, than I have done in my thirty plus years.

My mother used to say, 'Prevention is better than cure,' which is good, but if one does not have the knowledge to prevent whatever is happening, I thank God we have the cure! There is a verse in the Bible where God says, 'My people perish because of lack of knowledge.' For years I was one of these people because I did not realise I could have a better quality of life with him. It is all there in his message, the Bible, but we need somebody to explain this to us. The Holy Spirit is great at showing us stuff, but how do we find out about the Holy Spirit? We need genuine teachers who know God's message and will share this truth with us. We need them to fill the pulpits and platforms of this nation; not just in churches, but in school halls, universities, council meetings, market squares, even Parliament! God's message needs to be heard, *not* a message of judgement, but of God's goodness and loving kindness. God wants *everybody* to know him and *none* to perish. These teachers and preachers do exist, and I personally know some that have encouraged me on my journey. Their valuable insight into the truth enabled me to find the correct path. I thank our God for them all.

Now my journey takes on a whole new outlook. I am able to call God 'Lord' because he has become the lord of my life. I am not confined to an insular, single-minded framework because I have discovered somebody is watching over me and loves me. I am not living with despair, loneliness or frustration as they have been replaced by hope, contentment and a sense of belonging. I have tapped into an incredible source of treasure that is transforming my life. It is empowering me in the face of resistance and saying, 'Hold on in there, don't quit.' I have a different route to take, but I have a guide and map-reader (the Holy Spirit) and cannot get lost ever again. I have found *the* way not *a* way. Jesus said, 'I am the way and the truth and the life,' (John 14:6). Whatever direction a person takes can influence their future; so boy, am I glad I have changed direction and am now heading the right way!

This may be my last chapter (do I hear a cheer?) but it is not the end of my journey. God spoke clearly to my heart in the spring of 2013, 'Tell your story. Share your journey with others. Mention the highs and lows and ups and downs. Then tell them about me and how you discovered the truth about me on your journey. Tell them why I created them and how much I love them. Especially how much I love them. Write it all down in a book.' Every one of us have our own journeys to make in this life. We each have a story to tell: funny, happy, good, bad, ugly and sad. We can *all* write a book. Although not everyone's life has a sense of purpose or a happy ending. Some die in the depths of despair, others at the hands of a cruel dictator. Some have families round their deathbed, others lie dying in the gutter from a drug overdose. We are all going to die one day, this is the *one* thing we do agree on. The most important thing we need to hear, see and receive before we die, is the truth that *only* Jesus can bring us. Whether we hear this truth on our deathbed or as a young child, it does not matter. It is what we *do* with this truth that matters. Hold on to it and never let it go. Whoever calls on the name of Jesus shall be saved. Jesus is the only name that counts. Acts 4:12 says, 'Salvation is found in no one else, for there is no other name under heaven given to mankind by which we must be saved.' The world's ways and systems will fail one day, nothing is going to last. Everything will dissolve and become obsolete. Only Jesus can be our survival kit. *Only believe.*

Acknowledgements

Throughout my book, I have not mentioned the names of family, friends, churches or ministries for two reasons. First and most importantly, I respect their privacy; secondly, I wanted to keep the focus on a faithful God. I esteem him with the highest honour, and I thank him for bringing these people into my life. There were times on my journey when I felt so alone, but God carried me through those times, put me back on my feet and brought people into my life. You will know if you are one of those people, I do not have to name you! You are all such a blessing and I pray that God will continue to protect and bless you and your families. Many of you know Jesus, but some of you do not. I pray that as you read this book you will find room in your hearts for him.

I am grateful to my four wonderful sons who are now men out there in that challenging world. If I had never borne such fine sons, I would never have embarked on my quest for truth. In Christ you will never walk alone, he will provide far more for you than I ever could. I love you and am proud of you all.

There are others who have encouraged me to write this book, and help print, proof and photocopy stuff; others who 'felt led' to give me money (which helped finance my books, but they did not know that at the time!) and others who have given me wise advice about the publishing market.

I also want to express my gratitude to all the people who are presently in our lives in a professional role. For years it was extremely difficult to take Reuben to the hairdressers, dentist, doctor, etc.; even travelling on public transport, and shopping to try on new clothes and shoes was a struggle. Some years ago I prayed for a breakthrough in this area. One by one, God brought people into our lives that have walked the extra mile with us. So from the lady who cuts Reuben's hair and her husband who chauffeurs us around in his taxi; to the very patient dentist and doctor, and the podiatrist who comes to our home, I say a great big thank you!

Last, but not least, I just want to say a great big thank you to my publishers for all their hard work and endless energy—they have been amazingly patient with me!

Also a special mention to one particular young lady in the offices of Sprintprint (oops!) during the very early days of my writing; you gave me so much encouragement and help.

However, to be honest, without God's support I would never have ventured so far or achieved so much. This support is for everyone if they would *only believe.*

About the Author

Georgina Fletcher was born and brought up in Malvern and now lives in South Gloucestershire. She has kept personal journals of stories and poems since she was a young girl, many covering real life issues. *Only Believe* presents Georgina's personal story from fear of life itself to faith in an amazing God. Georgina has also written *Over the Hills and Far Away*, a collection of poems, and is presently completing a set of children's stories. If you found this book thought-provoking, funny, or just an enjoyable read, please let Georgina know, she would love to hear your comments. E-mail: gfletcher961@outlook.com Tel: 01454 602600.